BE THE BOSS

Turn a Four-Letter Word Into Highly Effective Leadership

By

Randy Maus

 **RESULTS PRESS**

Results Press
Unit 229
#180, 8601 Lincoln Blvd.
Los Angeles, California
90045

www.theresultspress.com

ISBN: 978-1-953089-81-6

First Edition

Copyright © 2021 by Randy Maus

All rights reserved. No part of this book may be reproduced in any form without the prior writer permission from the publisher. The opinions and conclusions drawn in this book are solely those of the author. The author and publisher bear no liability in connection with the use of the ideas presented.

Table of Contents

PROLOGUE

SECTION ONE – MINDSET: THINK LIKE A LEADER

- 1. You Know It When You See It 12
- 2. Hard Versus Soft Skills 14
- 3. See Yourself as a Leader 16
- 4. Know the Difference Between Confidence, Arrogance, and Humility 21

SECTION TWO – THE HARD TRUTHS OF LEADERSHIP

- 5. Your Team Wants You to Lead 27
- 6. You Are Not Equals 28
- 7. You Will Be Judged. Get Used to It. 30

SECTION THREE – SHAPING YOUR MINDSET

- 8. Multiple Ways of Doing 35
- 9. Choose Your Language 37
- 10. Useless Words 39
- 11. Samurai Poker – What Options Do You Have When You Accept Failure? 52
- 12. Prepare for Constant Change 55
- 13. The Learning Process 60
- 14. What If It's Not About You? 64
- 15. Receiving Feedback and Recognition 66

SECTION FOUR – UNDERSTANDING AND MOVING FORWARD

- 16. The Myth of Being Self-Made 69
- 17. The Thrive Curve 71
- 18. Moving from Hustle and Grind to Business Professional 73
- 19. See Yourself Beyond Where You Currently Are 78
- 20. As You Change, the World Around You Changes 79

SECTION FIVE – SKILLS: ACT LIKE A LEADER

21. CLARITY 81
22. ASK 82
23. LISTEN 89
24. ACKNOWLEDGE 95
25. DECIDE 97
26. MAKING DECISIONS – THE INFINITY OF EVERY DECISION 97
27. MANAGE THE GRAY 103
28. LIVING IN A WORLD WHERE YOU DON'T HAVE TO BE RIGHT 104
29. DEAL WITH THE BIG STUFF 105
30. WHAT YOU VALUE IS WHAT YOU EXPECT 107
31. USE STORIES TO COMMUNICATE YOUR VALUES 110
32. MANAGE UP 113
33. CREATE YOUR OWN CAREER PLAN 118
34. TREAT EVERYONE LIKE THEY ARE A MEMBER OF YOUR TEAM 121
35. ALWAYS LOOK FOR TALENT 123
36. NEVER TAKE ON SOMEONE ELSE'S PROBLEM 128
37. OWNERSHIP OF COMMUNICATION 133
38. SINS VERSUS MISTAKES 137
39. KNOW THE DIFFERENCE BETWEEN WHINING AND COMPLAINING .. 140
40. BRINGING PURPOSE, PRODUCTIVITY, AND MEANING BACK TO MEETINGS 142
41. START WITH AN IDEA 150
42. A FEW TIPS FOR BEING MORE EFFICIENT 153
43. NETWORKING. IT'S NOT JUST FOR NEW JOBS. 161
44. DOWNLOAD YOUR THOUGHTS 163
45. THE BENEFITS OF PRACTICE 166
46. THE ONE-STEP METHOD TO GETTING STARTED 169
47. AVOID "HEY, BUDDY" SYNDROME 170
48. OFFICE MORALE 178
49. FUN 181
50. OVERCOME POWER OVER 183
51. BE NICE 185
52. PEOPLE NEED STRUCTURE, NOT STRICTURE 186
53. COACH YOUR SUCCESSOR 190

54. GET OUTSIDE HELP	192
55. COACHING FOR ADVANCED SUCCESS	193
56. BE THE BOSS	203

APPENDIX

57. LEADING DURING CHALLENGING TIMES	204
58. A COMMON LEADERSHIP CHALLENGE	208

FURTHER READING AND RESOURCES ... 214

Prologue

The Leadership Gap

Leadership is the most powerful way to influence a group of individuals to achieve extraordinary outcomes. Why is it that there is such a challenging shortage of strong leadership in our organizations? It all comes down to our first job.

Think back to your first paid job. Perhaps you were in high school or just graduated. Did you babysit, deliver papers, or work at fast food behind the counter? I myself was a dishwasher at a country club. I held the privilege of cleaning all the plates from the various weddings, dances, and other events held at the club. Was I hired for my leadership skills or potential? NO! My boss cared that I showed up to work for my shift and cleaned the dishes as I was expected to do. Most jobs are like this. We are hired for a technical skill. By technical, I mean any skill needed in the organization.

Let's continue to explore the evolution of my dishwashing job. If I came into work and did a good job, they may offer me a job helping prep the food (peel potatoes and such). If I do this well, I may be promoted to work the line as a cook. If I continue to do well, I may now be asked to lead the cooks and run the kitchen. This is where it gets really challenging.

Up to this point, I have been developing my own technical skill. As soon as I am asked to lead others, the gap becomes apparent. All this time, I've been developing my technical skills, not my leadership skills. Leadership is an entirely different skillset. Knowing how to cook a medium-rare steak does not make me proficient in leading a team to produce multiple perfectly cooked steaks to serve a 500-person wedding reception.

Leaders in most organizations are given their positions because they have grown technically. It may not be dishwashing and culinary skills. For you, it may be skills related to drafting, nursing, construction, business consulting, software development, pharmacy and medicine, finance, logistics, or any of a multitude of competencies. As you gained professional experience and technical expertise, what opportunities did you have to develop your leadership skills?

If you are a new leader or facing challenges with your current team, you may experience a leadership gap. This happens when your technical skills are far advanced compared to your leadership skills. This book is designed to help you close that gap.

The book is separated into three main parts. The first focuses on building a leadership mindset. It's important to see yourself as a leader, and this section will help you do that. The next section is a series of tools effective leaders use in getting their work done. These are practical, applicable skills that can be used anywhere regardless of your working environment. The final section is dedicated to your continuing development and evolution as a leader.

Thank you for the opportunity to help you evolve as a leader, and thank you for applying your wisdom, experience, and learning toward improving our world.

Section One – Mindset: Think Like a Leader

"Our deepest fear is not that we are inadequate. Our deepest fear is that we are powerful beyond measure. It is our light, not our darkness that most frightens us. We ask ourselves, Who am I to be brilliant, gorgeous, talented, fabulous? Actually, who are you not to be? You are a child of God. Your playing small does not serve the world. There is nothing enlightened about shrinking so that other people won't feel insecure around you. We are all meant to shine, as children do. We were born to make manifest the glory of God that is within us. It's not just in some of us; it's in everyone. And as we let our own light shine, we unconsciously give other people permission to do the same. As we are liberated from our own fear, our presence automatically liberates others."

— Marianne Williamson

This has long been my favorite quote. It is powerful and providential. It speaks to our ability to have a great impact, no matter our circumstances. Indeed, we serve others when we live big. It allows others to rise and bring more of themselves into the world.

As a leader, this is you. The more you shine, the more your team has permission to shine. Bring your best and allow your team to do the same. Be visionary. Be vulnerable. Bring all of yourself to your leadership, and this will allow your team to shine with you – brightly.

1. You Know It When You See It

What is leadership?

When I start a talk or a coaching relationship, I ask people what leadership is. Most can't explain it, but they know it when they see it. If I ask who they think of as good leaders, they will give me examples from their lives. When I ask them what makes the person they mentioned a good leader, they first tell me that the person is a natural or born leader.

Saying that someone is a natural or born leader is not a compliment. It is like saying someone is an "overnight success." This overlooks and undervalues the hard work that the person has put into becoming the leader they are today. They have, consciously or unconsciously, been practicing skills their whole life that contribute to the leadership abilities they are displaying right now.

When someone uses this phrase, they are not really talking about the leader who seems like a "natural." They are really creating an excuse for themselves to bow out of the work required to become a stronger leader. Instead of focusing on developing their skills, they can think to themselves, *I'm not a natural-born leader, so I don't need to try or practice to become a better leader.*

There have been leaders for as long as there have been people. What is a leader? A leader is the person who brings a group of people together to work toward a common goal. Doesn't that sound easy? Simple? In the end, this is what a leader does. Why is it so challenging? It's hard because leaders have to develop a range of unseen skills whereas, in many other professions, you can see the skills being developed and applied.

A great example of this is my friend Chris, who is a carpenter.

He learned how to cut, shape, and finish wood. Whether he was building a table or installing trim along a baseboard, the product of his work was easy to see. In fact, the process and progress of his work are easy to observe. I can watch as he measures, cuts, and nails in each piece of wood. I can make judgements about the quality of his work, though not with the practiced eye his instructor may have had when he apprenticed. Chris himself can see the results of his work and self-critique in order to become better and refine his skills.

The biggest difference between what Chris does and what a leader does is that Chris and those around him understand the final product, what it should look like, and how to measure the quality of it. At the end of the process, a table should look like a table. Furthermore, there is a defined process of learning that Chris followed to acquire the skills for his profession. Ironically, this is not how most leaders are developed.

Most leaders are promoted into positions of leadership because they were good at a technical skill of some kind. They were proficient and worked well enough so that at some point they were offered a leadership position in their company. This is when the pain starts.

Now they are the manager. What they weren't told is that there is an entirely different skillset they need to develop – LEADERSHIP SKILLS. Organizations focus on the development and advancement of people with great technical skills without understanding the need to develop leadership skills at the same time. Now the person is a manager. They have great technical skills, but they have not practiced the skills required to lead a group of people to accomplish their business goals.

Fortunately, leadership is a set of skills that can be learned. Through practice and reflection, leaders are able to learn how to lead, understand how their strengths contribute to their leadership style, and close the leadership gap.

Familiar, but Uncomfortable

Take a moment and find someone nearby—roommate, workmate, spouse, friend, random stranger. Ask to shake hands with them. Shake their hand. Now ask them to shake hands again, but hold out your other hand, the one you don't usually use for shaking hands. I'm guessing the first shake felt familiar and comfortable where the second handshake was probably familiar, but uncomfortable.

This is a great example of leadership. We have experienced leadership all our lives. When we see it, it feels familiar. Yet, when we try to lead, it can feel uncomfortable. This discomfort comes from our lack of practice in using leadership skills. The good news is that we can get more comfortable as we practice the skills required to lead and gain experience leading others.

If you are growing as a leader, remember that everyone contributes in their own way. Some will want to grow to be amazing leaders like you. Others will produce fantastic work without ever desiring to manage others. As a leader, you can still bring all of these people together to achieve amazing success.

2. Hard Versus Soft Skills

I have often heard the term "hard skills versus soft skills", which caused me to wonder where the phrase originated. From what I could find, the concept of hard skills versus soft skills originates in the U.S. army. As you can imagine, this is an organization dedicated to training, as they have a constant supply of new recruits. The phrase was used to denote "hard" skills as technical skills and "soft" skills as interpersonal skills—both considered important in military affairs.

After this idea was introduced in 1972, it became ubiquitous across North America and used globally.

I grew up associating "hard" with "tough, committed, and all in", whereas "soft" meant "weak, wimpy, and lazy." I never liked this phrase as to me it set up a false dichotomy where technical skills somehow rated better than interpersonal skills. It wasn't until I was speaking to my spouse that she offered a new perspective. Her interpretation was that it makes sense to call the interpersonal skills "soft" skills because the skills you use to influence others are often required to be done in a soft way.

I reflected on this immensely and see the wisdom of this point of view. "Soft" can have many meanings. I was interpreting it to mean weak; however, I may have misinterpreted. My spouse's interpretation was a great view of how we use our interpersonal skills to get things done. The most effective leaders don't hammer their people in a hard way, time and time again. They often use softer approaches that draw out the best in others.

This is illustrated in the Tai Chi exercise called Push Hands. It is a graceful exchange where two people are moving back and forth while constantly connected. The object is not to literally push someone across the room. The goal is to connect and allow energy to flow between you. If you push too hard, you will push the other person away and lose connection. Contrarily, if you offer no resistance, you lose connection. Therefore, you need to be soft and firm at the same time. Prior to this, I'd always seen these two words as opposites. Practicing Push Hands, I realized that they aren't opposites. Instead, they are different and complementary.

Another example of this is partner, or ballroom, dancing. I used to think that the leader had to make all the decisions and communicate them through a strong posture and powerful movements. As it turns out, dancing is a partnership and requires both partners to be soft and firm. If one partner is too forceful, it disrupts the flow. If the other partner is not firm enough in their posture, it is difficult to communicate through their bodies as they move.

Though hard skills are useful and important, soft skills are now recognized more broadly and tend to have a greater impact on professional advancement and project success. As a leader, how can you adjust your style to be firm and soft at the same time and bring together the hard and soft skills in your team and yourself?

3. See Yourself as a Leader

Identity is a core part of being human. Hence when someone has an "identity crisis" it is a major life event. Yet, our identity is an adaptable and changing construct.

We start out as children and we think of ourselves as a son or daughter. Depending on our family, we may add brother, sister, cousin to that list. In a few years, we enter school and add "student" to our identity along with "friend." We enter a workplace and see ourselves as an "employee." These are a few of the many labels we use to identify ourselves as people.

To be a leader is to take the next step. Saying it is a step doesn't do it justice. It is more of a leap, yet it is critical and the first place to start in growing as a leader.

Step 1

Your first step to seeing yourself as a leader is to realize—YOU ARE NOT AN IMPOSTER!

You were chosen specifically to take on this role and you agreed to it.

Many years ago, Alfred Adler created the concept that has come to be known as Imposter Syndrome—a belief system in which a person does not believe they are worthy of some task, experience, or position. It stems from a lack of confidence and the negative thought that someone else is surely meant to be doing this rather than me.

You may not think you are qualified for your job, relationship, task, project, responsibility as a parent or leader. The good news is that this is completely irrelevant. Whatever position you have, you have it. It is yours to fulfill. You call the shots. You make the decisions. Whether you see yourself as an imposter or someone ready to take on the responsibility, either way, you are the leader, and your team will look to you.

A real imposter is someone who dishonestly presents themselves as someone or something other than who they really are. The con artist, the fake Facebook account, the spy are all examples of imposters—people who intentionally deceive others about their identity or purpose.

In actuality, no one is an imposter. If you are in your job, relationship, volunteer opportunity, etc. and you are honest about who you are and your qualifications, you are NOT an imposter. You are the right person to be in this position at this moment, and it is your chance to make the most of it.

I once worked with a keen new professional named Charlene. She was very sharp and exceedingly humble—so humble that she was overwhelmed by everyone around her and overlooked her own gifts and potential to contribute. I talked to her about the reasons she was hired into the position. She could not be an imposter because we chose her, and she chose us. There were no backup options if she chose not to fulfill the job because she was the authentic person we wanted to take on the role. It's important to remember that you are not replacing someone. You are not expected to perform in the same way your predecessor did. In fact, you are often chosen to expand and take the work further. Embrace that you are the one in the role. Own it.

Step 2

The second step is to let go of what your predecessor(s) did. It simply doesn't matter. They are not here. You are not living in their shadow. Even if they were outstanding, the organization doesn't want another one of them. They want you and what you can bring to the organization.

If you are not sure what you bring, I want you to approach two or three current or past colleagues and ask them what you do well or what they value about you. Come back and write it down here.

What colleagues have told me they value about me:

_____
_____
_____
_____
_____

Step 3

See yourself as THE leader.

Who do you want to be as a leader?

Now that you know who you want to be as a leader, how does a leader like you act? What do they do?

Knowing that you are the leader you want to be, choose to act in the way you expect a leader like you to behave. What results will this give you?

So many people focus on what they want to have—a trusting team, exceeding expectations on a regular basis, good communication between colleagues, the ability to speak in front of a group succinctly and without terror, etc. They think they have to have these abilities prior to being the leader they want to be. In fact, the process is exactly reversed. Instead, they need to identify the leader they want to be. This makes it easier to focus training efforts on the actions that will make them into the leader they want to be so that finally they can have the team, performance, results they desire.

Who do I want to be as a leader?

_____
_____
_____
_____

What actions does a leader like me do?

_____
_____
_____
_____

What results will I have when I perform the activities a leader like me performs?

_____
_____
_____
_____

What if what you see now was always possible?

In addition to seeing yourself as the leader, see your team as the team you want it to be. See your organization as the organization you want it to be. See your business as the business you want it to be.

It is easy to focus on who I am right now as a leader rather than who I want to be. Likewise, it is easy to focus on the organization we are right now, rather than the organization we want to be. How we see ourselves now affects how we will grow. It's easy to understand what we are, but not what we can be. Organizations are similar and want to be something different, more, better, etc. The trap is that we continue to operate from the present-day mindset instead of operating as though we were already living that future.

An example may help. I was working with a client who wanted to grow his business to 200 people when he employed around 50 at present. I asked him what does a 200-person company look like in your field? How does it operate? What are its revenues and expenses? What markets does it serve? What is the organizational structure? I wanted him to stop thinking that he runs a 50-person company and instead change his mindset so that he sees himself as CEO of a 200-person company that currently employs 50 people. Moving your mind to operate from a future state will affect the decisions you make as you train and focus your mind to create your real goal, rather than focusing on the current state of the company. If you focus on what you currently have, you will get more of it. To move forward, you need to train your mind to think as though you are already in your future reality.

4. Know the Difference Between Confidence, Arrogance, and Humility

Being able to honestly assess yourself and your colleagues is an important trait for a leader. You'll notice that I put assessing yourself first. Most leaders misunderstand the difference between three key virtues that allow you to lead from a place of self-assuredness.

Leading is a brave activity. Not everyone is willing to stand up and lead.

Leading is a vulnerable activity. Not everyone is comfortable taking on the responsibility to make a situation better, knowing that others will have an opinion about what they are saying and doing.

Therefore, it is important to understand the differences in confidence a leader may experience. This same concept applies more broadly to an entire team. Consider what you learn in this section about the Spectrum of Confidence. What level of confidence do you have in yourself as a leader? What is the level of confidence your team members have in each other as a team?

Self-Abuse –

The action of unfairly criticizing yourself

Have you or someone you know ever awkwardly deflected a compliment? On the self-abuse end of the spectrum, leaders do not understand or appreciate their strengths. There is great discomfort in accepting their role in achievements and the success of the group.

Self-abuse does not serve the leader who may wrongly think they are being humble. In fact, this can undermine a leader's position within the team. Further, it may do harm in terms of your team's confidence in each other or for recognition of your team for their efforts by senior leaders.

Demonstrating a complete lack of confidence is one thing, but those with lower self-esteem often take this another step and undermine their own contributions, efforts, or credibility through self-abuse.

Humility –

Understanding that your contributions are part of a team effort and recognizing that what you achieve is reliant upon the contributions of your coworkers or teammates

I have seen too many people mistake self-abuse for humility. Humility is not denying your gifts, skills, and contributions. Humility is understanding that your contributions are part of a team effort and recognizing that what you achieve is reliant upon the contributions of your coworkers or teammates as much as your own efforts. Putting yourself down or denying your contributions does not make you look humble. It makes you look weak. True humility isn't disparaging yourself but reminding others of the efforts of all the people involved.

Confidence –

The feeling or belief that one can rely on someone or something; firm trust

Most people mistake arrogance for confidence. Confidence is the ability to say I am good at something without feeling guilty or shy, and immediately trying to take it back. Confidence is stating that your team operates effectively in whatever functional areas apply. It is not arrogant to say that you are good at something. It is arrogant to say I am better than everyone else at something.

It does not serve your team or your organization to focus only on your weaknesses. If your team doesn't know what your strengths are, how will they understand how you can help them? If you hold back, the people around you will achieve less because you thought you were being modest when you were really afraid of judgement.

A great example of this occurs in the book *Bravo Two Zero* by Andy McNabb. He and his team of Special Air Services commandos were set behind enemy lines in the first Gulf War with Iraq to search and destroy SCUD missile launchers. In the course of their mission, circumstances changed drastically. The enemy found them. They were forced to flee, and they were a long way from allied forces. After finding a temporary refuge, they assessed their situation.

The weather had turned cold and snow began to fall. In this moment, they gathered as a team and each shared their current status. This is the most extreme situation a person could be in—deep in enemy territory with worsening weather conditions and wanting to stay alive while making it back to your allies. McNabb explains it well, that each person on his team had to give a realistic assessment of their condition. It was not time to "Be a hero" or "suck it up." Why? Because if a team member is not 100% realistic about their condition, this can put the rest of the team in jeopardy. For instance, one of his team injured his leg and shared that he was able to go on, but expected it to get worse if they had to run. Another team member was suffering from dehydration; this condition can be deadly if ignored. The team was open about their status, which helped them to plan their next steps.

Growing up with action movies like *Rambo* and *Commando*, where one lone hero saves the day while toughing out the pain and injury, I was surprised when I read this. It got me thinking, though, about how this concept applies to leadership, and I realized it is no different in any circumstance.

You need to give a realistic view of what you can provide, and this doesn't mean a negative view. It doesn't mean you downplay your abilities. It means being honest about your strengths as much as your drawbacks.

For most of us, we are our own worst critics. We can be hard on ourselves; harder than we are on others. Having confidence means we are able to share our shortcomings without adding the emotional weight of judgement. If you are not good with finances, own it. Don't call yourself worthless because it is not a strength. You are not able to do everything that occurs in your organization, nor are you meant to. Each person has their own strengths and weaknesses, which is why leadership is so special. It is bringing people together to maximize those strengths and counter those weaknesses in order to achieve something spectacular.

What are your strengths? Not sure? Ask three to five people you trust. (Of those people, only one should be a friend or family member.) Work to find others you work with in your organization or possibly business partners that will give you their open assessment of your strengths.

Cockiness –

The belief that you are good at what you do without the blindness of believing you have nothing more to learn

I love a team with a little bit of cockiness. I see this differently from arrogance, though. Cockiness displays a sense of confidence that you and your team are good at what you do without the arrogance of thinking you have nothing more to learn. A team that is a bit cocky believes in itself and its members' abilities while at the same time continuing to learn and challenge themselves to improve their services, products, and performance.

What experiences have you had with your team that demonstrate high achievement?

How often do you retell these stories to instill a sense of pride and accomplishment among the team?

In what ways do you tell your team they are doing well and how often?

Arrogance –

The belief that you are better than everyone else

Arrogance is thinking you have arrived at perfection. Arrogance is when you think you are better than everyone else. Arrogance is believing you have nothing more to learn. Arrogance is a cancer that will rot away all of your gains, for when you think you have reached the pinnacle that is when you fall behind. Others will move ahead. In fact, when you see arrogance in other companies that means opportunity for you.

Spectrum of Confidence

Self-Abuse	Humility	Confidence	Cockiness	Arrogance
Self-defeating Low self-esteem No recognition of strengths and contributions	Praise team members Avoid recognition Can accept a compliment	Communicates personal and team strengths as well as weaknesses	Know you are good at what you do Committed to getting better	Believe you are the best Blind to how others are improving

Section Two – The Hard Truths of Leadership

The challenge of leadership is to be strong, but not rude; be kind, but not weak; be bold, but not bully; be thoughtful, but not lazy; be humble, but not timid; be proud, but not arrogant; have humor, but without folly.

― *Jim Rohn*

5. Your Team Wants You to Lead

Many in leadership positions worry about what others will think about their decisions. This can often hold them back from making a decision altogether, which is a big mistake. When the leader refuses to make a decision, it is like putting the entire team on pause. They are now working in limbo as they need a clear direction from you and they are not getting it. Instead of gaining respect or positive regard, the team only gets frustrated and loses faith in their leader. You can always come back from a bad decision, but you have to make a decision first. Without a decision, there is no action. Without action, there are no results.

Remember that your team wants you to lead. They want you to guide them when guidance is needed. They want you to decide when a decision is needed. They want you to challenge them when the challenge will make them grow. They like that you are responsible, and they look to you for responsibility. Though leadership can at times be daunting, overwhelming, or even frightful, never fear to lead. Your team desires your leadership, and they are depending on it.

6. You Are Not Equals

You can do what I cannot do. I can do what you cannot do. Together we can do great things.

— *Mother Teresa*

I was mentoring a keen newer leader. When I asked him about his leadership style, he said that he wants his team to see him as their equal. I believe he said, "I want my staff to know that we are all the same." I understand where this sentiment comes from, and I appreciate that it is said with care. The truth is that it is wholly inaccurate and undermined his leadership.

You are not the same as your staff. The truth is, you are not equals.

I gave my friend one example that proved this point. I asked him if his team could fire him from his job. He thought for a second and replied, "No." Then you are not equal. As their leader, you carry a different level of responsibility and authority than your team members. Moreover, they don't see you as their peer. They see you as their boss. They want you to be their leader. Otherwise, it's like a family where the parents want to be buddies with their children instead of the mother or father that the children need them to be.

This doesn't mean you are better than the members of your team. Sometimes leaders confuse this. Each person on your team brings their own strengths and special contributions. They will be better than you are at various tasks. If they aren't, you're not hiring the best.

Though you are not equal in your responsibility, you and each member of your team have value. Acting as their leader, you are able to recognize and bring those talents together, make the decisions needed to move forward, and act from a place of confidence without believing you are better or lesser than anyone else.

When leaders use the phrase that all people are the same, it is a complete misnomer in concept. What we need to say is that we all have value as people though we do not share the same responsibility. My staff members don't want to be the same as me because they don't want to carry the responsibility I do. They like having someone who will make the final call when times get challenging. It's OK to include people in decision-making, but never assume you are the same. If you were in the same circumstance, you wouldn't be leading this group. You would be one of their peers.

In Christianity, Jesus is a seminal figure in the teachings of that faith. Jesus was not an equal with his disciples. He was their leader, teacher, and servant. They didn't follow him because he was the same as everyone else. They followed him because he was different. He valued everyone equally though he and each person had a different role to play. Your name may not be Jesus (though maybe it is), but your situation is the same. You are not in the same position as each of your colleagues, but you are each valued for how you contribute to the work you are doing.

Accepting the differences between being a leader and the people you lead is a big step. Understand that you are not better than the people you work with, nor are you the same. Each person has value and each leader carries the responsibility that their team relies on them to carry.

7. You Will Be Judged. Get Used to It.

As the leader, the spotlight is on you, especially if you are a new leader. Your team wants to know all about you because they want to know what having you around means for them. It is instinctual to assess new leaders and wonder whether you can trust them.

Having others look to you for guidance and direction is part of the job of being a leader. It is the relationship between the leader and those who are led. The followers agree to do what is expected of them. The leader agrees to take responsibility for setting the direction of the team's efforts.

It is not easy being judged by others; but if you look at any leader in any business, community, or political position they are all highly visible positions to the people whom they lead. It doesn't make the observation any easier, but it will help you in your position to understand this.

Fortunately, there are ways to reduce the impact of this fact of leadership life.

First, connect with your team. When you first start in a leadership role with new colleagues, take time to connect with each one. Build the personal-professional connection that will assist you in moving forward.

Second, answer the questions that they are all asking. What does this mean for me? They also want to know what's next. Being new and learning about the organization, you may not have a clearly defined vision for where you will take the team, but you need to tell them what your plans are in the interim. Are you meeting with everyone to get a sense of organizational strengths and challenges? Are you consulting with your board of directors or others about the direction of the company? If you have a clear plan, what is it? Share whatever you have with your team. This will help them feel more at ease. Team members are least comfortable when they feel insecure because they don't know what is happening. As a leader, you have a great opportunity to reduce this fear for them while at the same time improving your connection to the team you lead.

Third, remember that your team wants you to lead. You are in a position of tremendous influence because they are looking to you for direction.

When I was younger, I watched a show called *Tour of Duty* that took place during the US-Vietnam war. It focused on a team of soldiers who received a new lieutenant to lead them. Their new leader was not warmly welcomed and at the time I could not understand why. Surely, he was their leader. Why didn't they accept him as such? He had the rank.

What he didn't have was their respect. Unlike the average work situation, their lives literally depended on his ability to lead the group effectively. They wanted to know if he could be trusted with their lives. As he got to know them, give clear orders, and show that he valued their lives, he earned their trust—and they followed willingly.

Knowing you will be judged; it is important to stay aware of your motivation. It is easy to look to your team or your boss for accolades and praise. It's much like a student wanting good grades in school. The only problem is that this gives you an external locus of control, which is usually impossible to live up to.

It's like being a student. If all you seek is a grade, your self-esteem will always be dictated by the teacher. Similarly, if in your leadership role, you seek to please your team, supervisor, board, or other person involved in your business, you will crumble under the myriad expectations.

Instead, make your choices for yourself and know and respect your own performance. If you are receiving feedback, it does not diminish the value of that feedback. Take it with confidence, understanding that the other person has offered their opinion. If it is specific to your work and actions, it probably has merit. If it is a general or judgmental comment, it probably has much less legitimacy. Choose to live your own life instead of being constantly shaped by the whims of those around you. Being judged isn't easy, but it comes with the job. Know who you are and lead with confidence, understanding that other people's judgements aren't worthy of or relevant to you.

Respect is Earned. Power is Taken.

As a kid, I looked at royal families and thought about rulership by divine right. This is the rationale royalty used to justify their positions in society. Rule by divine right meant that they were sanctioned by God to rule the land.

This concept never seemed right to me. Somebody had to be the first ruler and this family retained power. That is, they retained power until another family came and knocked them off or another kingdom conquered them. Therefore, they weren't ruling because of God's favor. It was because their ancestor was the most recent champion to take the throne.

I don't advocate violence, nor have I had the privilege of coaching royalty yet, but the ancestors of royalty set an interesting example. They ruled because they expected to rule. Others gave them power over them to rule. It's not that different in a team.

You have to earn someone's respect, but you take power by the way you act and the expectation you set. People gravitate toward the person who will make decisions and assign them tasks. If I ask you to do something and you do it, you've given me power over you. This is not a manipulative or evil action. It is a common agreement we see in our businesses, workplaces, and communities between the organization and the employee. In fact, there is comfort in hierarchy. See yourself as their leader and set your expectations accordingly. Take the power you need to be successful. Being a leader is recognizing your personal power and using it to the best effect for your team, organization, and customers.

You Don't Have to Apologize for Doing Your Job

Being a leader means that you will be engaged in many uncomfortable moments. A major reason for this is that it is your responsibility to develop your team, improve your organization, and enhance your results. This requires growth, and growth comes with discomfort. As you are helping your organization to grow, it means you will go through uncomfortable situations with your team. In fact, it <u>requires</u> you to have uncomfortable conversations with your team.

When feeling uncomfortable about pushing others to grow, it is easy to apologize. Yet, you never need to apologize for doing your job. This is different than admitting your mistakes. When you make a mistake, it is good to acknowledge it and share how you are correcting it. Apologies are admittance of wrongdoing. If you have wronged someone on the team, then apologize. It makes sense. However, if you are giving feedback, calling a meeting, or disciplining someone, these actions don't require an apology. You are just doing your job.

Section Three – Shaping Your Mindset

You can't start the next chapter of your life if you keep re-reading the last one.

— *Michael McMillian*

8. Multiple Ways of Doing

When taking on a leadership role it is common to question if you are "doing it right." You may be curious about how other leaders or their teams operate. You may be seeking models to emulate with your own team.

In the process of discovery, you will find multiple examples. When seeking information, other leaders will share their models with you. Remember to ensure that whatever you decide works for you and your team in your given circumstance. Other leaders are sharing the experiences, decisions, and activities they used when engaging with their teams; but, the circumstances, team members, and work culture were all different from your current situation. No two workplaces are the same. Knowing this, you can use what works for you and adapt it to your team culture and leadership style. There are multiple ways to achieve our goals. Another person's way may not be the best option for you, but you can still learn from them.

A great example of this is the movie *Cool Runnings* about the 1988

Olympic bobsled team from Jamaica. This team is looking for a way to win. The leader especially feels the pressure and decides to mimic the best team in the competition—the Swiss. He goes to the extent of having his team count off in German (einz, zwei, drei) to start their race.

The first run is disastrous. The team barely gets into the sled in time. On the way down, they careen and bounce off the walls of the course, resulting in a last place finish. The team is sad and despondent. Though they have learned from watching the Swiss team, copying the Swiss team did not make them successful.

That night the team is meeting to discuss what to do next. One of the team members stands up to declare that this is a Jamaican team, and they need to be Jamaican, not Swiss, in how they compete.

The next day, the team walks to the starting blocks. Instead of counting off in German, the leader speaks out a starting poem/phrase. It speaks to them as Jamaicans and is more aligned with who they are and their culture. It inspires them and they achieve amazing results as they go from last place in the standings to finishing eighth overall.

"Feel the rhythm! Feel the rhyme! Get on up, it's bobsled time! Cool Runnings!"

How much different does this starting phrase sound than einz, zwei, drei? Both achieve the same purpose in focusing the team at the start of the race and aligning their efforts. Yet, just as the Swiss starting phrase didn't work for Jamaica, I imagine the Jamaican start phrase would not work well for the Swiss, either.

In having a starting phrase, the Jamaican's may have copied the Swiss, but it wasn't until they made it their own that they were successful. Working with your team will be much the same. You may learn of a wonderful leadership technique. Apply it, but remember to apply it as *you* would apply it. Have integrity with yourself and your business environment. There are many great ideas, and there is much that can be learned from others. But it must be applied using your own unique flavor.

There are numerous examples in business of a strategy that was copied from one company to another but it failed. The strategy may be useful, but the transition failed to take into account the unique elements of the second company such as its team dynamic, values, purpose, and culture. A strategy, process, or procedure doesn't exist outside of the people who bring it to life. Because people are so diverse, this creates many ways of taking advantage of new ideas. Understand this to customize ingenuity in your work environment.

Your way may not be their way, but it might be the right way for you.

9. Choose Your Language

Language is the tool we use for thinking and connecting. That is why it is so important to choose your language. Many people are afraid to ask of others, and this leads to very weak language. Understand that I am not advocating for terse or impolite language. As I learned in Tai Chi, you can be soft and firm in the same moment. When I speak of strong versus weak language, I am highlighting the difference between communicating clearly and with expectation versus allowing confusion to dominate your conversations.

Example...

Weak Language: Would anyone like to take on this project?

Strong Language: Who will take on this project?

As a leader, it is OK to have expectations of others. There is no need to shy away from this. High performers like expectations, and strong language allows them to best understand what is expected of them.

Weak language creates confusion, avoids accountability, and predictably achieves poor results.

If you change the language you use from the language of request to the language of expectation, how does this change your interactions?

Activity

This week record 2 or 3 conversations with the people you lead. Before doing so, be sure to tell them what you are doing and ask permission. You want them to know that you are using it for your own development and that the recordings will not be shared beyond your coach (if you are using one) and yourself.

Set aside some time to listen to or watch the recording. Pay close attention to the words you use and how you present ideas to your colleagues. Is your language clear? Is it assertive, passive, or aggressive? How does the other person respond verbally and physically to what you are sharing?

Recording ourselves is one of the best tools we can use. More than someone telling us what we are doing, we can see it for ourselves. When reviewing the footage, remember not to be too hard on yourself. Instead, look for how you might improve your language to improve your interactions.

Life Is Not Fair, So Don't Choose Unlucky

Annie Duke, author of *Thinking in Bets: Making Smarter Decisions When You Don't Have All the Facts,* has analyzed decision-making, and she noticed something powerful. Poker players who avoid using the words unfair and unlucky tend to perform better. When a person thinks a circumstance was unfair or unlucky, they are less likely to reflect on the decision that led them to that outcome. Therefore, they don't learn, and this means they will repeat or exacerbate the mistake. If you see the situation as unlucky or unfair, it moves accountability away from you; but it does not serve you as a way to grow from the experience.

10. Useless Words

Language is exceedingly powerful. It is so powerful because it is the machine code of our mind. It is the programming language we use to tell our brain what to do. Like a computer language, an error in the words you use can mess up your entire mental program. In a lifetime of coaching others, I have found a few words that I consider truly evil (or at least pretty useless). Whenever you use these words, you lose power, accountability, and credibility.

Maybe

Can you feel a shudder as you read this word? Maybe is quite possibly the most useless word in the English language. What does it communicate? Answer: nothing!

When I was young, I quickly figured out what the word "maybe" really means. It means "no."

When you ask someone if they want to get together, go for a coffee, attend an event, work on a project, etc. and they say maybe, what they really mean is "no." To this day, I have not had anyone tell me maybe when that actually turned into a yes or some other kind of committed action.

People who use the word maybe may believe this is a softer, kinder way of turning another person down. It is a safe "out" to try to avoid potential hurt feelings. Instead, it achieves exactly the opposite—frustration and distrust.

A firm answer is much better than a weak answer like "maybe." When responding with "maybe", it wastes other people's time. Worse, if they were counting you as a yes, now you have lost trust with them as you didn't follow through on their request.

"Maybe" is easy to misinterpret. Some people will read this as "yes", others as "no", and still others as "they are unsure and will get back to me." This is another reason you are set up to fail when using this word. If I interpret it differently than you do, we are bound to have mismatched expectations.

I recommend eliminating this word from your language. It is a weak way of saying no. For some reason, people assume it softens the no by saying "maybe." Instead, what it really does is build hope. When that hope is dashed later, it erodes trust in the relationship—trust that would still be present if you had only replied "no" instead of "maybe."

If you need to soften your answer, first give a definite yes or no. You can then follow this by letting them know you will follow up with them if circumstances change. Most people understand this as schedules and commitments can be fluid.

Here are some considerations to replace this word in your vocabulary.

> "Consider me a no for right now and I will get back to you if I change my mind."
>
> "Thanks for inviting me to participate. I'm not able to right now, but I will let you know if something changes."

What words will you use in place of "maybe?"

_____
_____
_____
_____

Warning: "Maybe" has the ability to disguise itself as other words. Watch out for "maybe" disguised as the following words. Add to the list any other words you hear in your interactions that mean "maybe."

        Possibly   Whatever

    _____   _____

    _____   _____

Should

Should, could, and would are all derivatives of the first word. They all imply intent without any substance. Furthermore, they add weight—the weight of guilt. On one hand, they are an easy way out. "I should have ..." is a way to self-flagellate without addressing the real issue. If you should have done something, why are you not doing something about it now? What did you learn and how are you applying it? Do you need to apologize to someone or have a meaningful conversation about an uncomfortable topic?

"Should" is a waste of energy. In looking back, it is a word meant to punish without adding the benefit of a lesson. It is remorse mixed with judgement that we apply to ourselves and others.

That's right, we don't beat only ourselves up using this language. I hear it applied often to other people in our lives. It is assumed that people know what you expect of them, or that they know what you value and will comport themselves accordingly. Here's the kicker—no one knows what is going on in your mind except you. Each person has their own values and expectations. On the surface, this seems obvious; yet over and over I hear people say that some other person should have done what they wanted them to do or should have known what they expected.

Where does the expectation come from? It comes from a person's worldview, values, and beliefs. How we see the world is how we expect others to see it. For that reason, we expect others to act how we would act. We expect them to make decisions the way we make decisions. That is why it is so flabbergasting when they choose a different option, disagree with us, or don't fulfill their commitments in the way we would.

When you understand that each person's experience is truly unique to that person and learn not to expect the same of them as you do yourself, you will seek to better understand the other person, and this will lead you to a much better relationship or understanding of the current situation.

Warning: "Should" has been adapted into many other words and phrases. It takes on a different look but carries the same meaning. For instance, they "ought to" get that report done.

Reflect on when you are using the word "should."

_____
_____
_____
_____
_____

When are others using the word "should?"

_____
_____
_____
_____

What alternate words do you or the people on your team use that have the same meaning and intent as "should?"

_____
_____
_____
_____

But

What people say after they use the word "but" is what they actually mean. Listen closely during your conversations and you will find this to be quite true. The word "but" is used as a buffer between a nice comment and our real thought. It is misused and intended as a softening blow before sharing what a person really thinks. It's understandable, as for most people how they are perceived by others is of utmost concern to them. They may want to share a contrary idea but worry about how it will be received.

In order to improve communication and interpret others better, there is a simple tool you can use. Replace the word "but" with the word "and." This simple word replacement will show you what is really being said.

Try

In the science fiction classic, *Star Wars V: The Empire Strikes Back*, the wizened teacher Yoda tells his pupil, "Do or do not do. There is no try." It may seem a little cheesy to quote a science fiction film character from the '80s, but the statement is entirely true.

When you think about it, we never "try" anything. We attempt to reach a goal and we either succeed or we don't. We can then use that result to alter our next attempt.

"Try" is a very weak word that sets us up for failure from its first use. The meaning of the word is like a built-in excuse for not achieving what we are "trying" to do. Consider how much effort you give a task when you say you will do it versus saying you will "try" to do it.

Avoid using this word by always planning to do something. Be specific and committed in your language. You may not achieve exactly what you set out to do, and that is OK. It is only failure. Failure is much better than the half commitment of "try." You can learn from it and make a better attempt next time.

If you're not convinced, consider the following scenario. You run into a friend or colleague whom you have not seen for some time. After an enjoyable short chat, you tell the other person, "We should get together for coffee sometime." Reflecting back on that scenario, how many times has this happened with zero results or follow up? This is like saying we'll "try" to get together. It results in never actually getting together.

If this is really important to you, I recommend taking advantage of the miracles of the modern world. With our mobile phones, we are blessed with being able to carry our calendars in our pockets. If someone ever tells you "we should get together for coffee sometime" instead of saying "yes", consider responding with something like the following.

"That sounds great. I'm available next Tuesday at 9 am, how does that work for you?"

"Good idea. Why don't we look at our calendars right now and schedule something?"

You can see the difference between intention and action. Changing a few words changes the entire interaction.

Steal

As in "I stole this person from you" (when referring to recruiting) or "Are you stealing our coffee?" (when someone is making themselves a cup), this indicates that you feel on some level that you or the other person did something wrong. You may worry about what the other person thinks or perhaps you feel somehow slighted by their actions. Either situation may make you uncomfortable and prompt joking about "stealing" something.

If others have benefited, never accuse them, even lightheartedly, about stealing from someone. It is negative and can harm the relationship when, really, it's based on your discomfort with a situation. Instead, be welcoming and congratulatory or invite a discussion on the topic. This will get you much further ahead.

Disappointed

Among children, which is to say among people, we all fall on the spectrum of rule-follower on one end and rule-breaker on the other. Growing up, I was more inclined to the rule-follower end of the spectrum. It worked well for me, but when I messed up the effect could be devastating.

Growing up, I was blessed with parents that loved me. They weren't draconic, but the few rules they had they expected to be obeyed. The number one rule was that our mother had to know where we were.

We visited friends all the time, and she was OK with that. But if we changed plans, she wanted to know. As a parent now myself, I appreciate the peace of mind it gives you to have some idea where your child is when they are away from home.

One time, I was hanging out with friends and we had decided to go to another friend's house. It was winter and pretty cold out. I was excited at spending time together and forgot to update my mom. My friends and I had a great time, but when I got home it wasn't very pleasant. She didn't beat me or berate me. She used something infinitely more powerful: the D word—disappointed. I would have preferred a spanking to hearing that word cross her lips. I felt shame, which if you've read any of Brene Brown, you appreciate how powerful it is. I vowed to never do that again, and my brother and sister each had similar experiences. Not many, but we can relate.

I bring this up not to promote shaming your teammates. In fact, shame, we have come to find, is a very negative practice in our work and private lives.

Instead, I bring this up to ensure you are mindful of the language you are using; if you choose to use this word with your team, understand that it has power. It is not something to use lightly or often. It can erode the relationships you have built and disengage the staff.

I'll Be Honest With You

What a horrid and useless phrase, with its many variations:

- To be honest, ...
- Honestly, ...
- Let me be truthful, ...
- Truthfully, ...
- I'll be honest with you ...

What are you saying when you use this phrase? Were you lying to me about everything else you told me? Should I question the validity of our previous discourse? What has prompted you to be honest with me now?

This phrase elicits any manner of questions and raises certain questions about what the person is sharing. Is this the intent? No, I don't believe it is. Why, then, is this phrase used so commonly?

There are a few reasons.

First, it is used to imply an intimacy with another person. Using this phrase indicates you are going to give more information than you normally would. You may want the other person to feel a special connection, and thereby listen more closely to you. You're showing them a privilege that others do not receive, and you're taking them into your trust.

Another reason is that we often hold back or share partial information. Think about when you were a child. Did you ever take more cookies than you knew you were allowed? Perhaps you weren't entirely truthful. It is not uncommon to hold back information to avoid looking bad.

Perhaps you want to "soften up" the person. By this, I mean relax them prior to delivering potentially unpleasant news. We are hard-wired to pay attention to another person's response. When we use the phrase "I'll be honest with you, …" already the other person's senses come to attention. They are listening and taking in all the details. Their initial response is a way to assess their initial reaction before you've given them any information. If you sense they will take the information badly, you may adjust what you have to say.

This phrase is also used to make you look like the good guy. "I'll be honest with you …" may imply that no one else is honest with you about the situation. Using this phrase, you can communicate that, though reluctant, you are the one willing to raise the unmentionable subject or share the bad news. You're the Good Samaritan bringing a dose of reality about the circumstance. Shouldn't you receive some acknowledgment for being honest?

The most common reason a phrase like this is used is that it is a habit. The phrase is used as a meaningless introduction without conscious thought as to what it really implies. It is similar to how we reply when someone asks us "How are you?" Our response does not engage our thinking brain. Instead, the automated part of our mind recognizes the phrase and provides a practiced response. In this case, the phrase can be damaging, as people might wonder about the veracity of what we've told them in the past.

In conversation, there is no need to tell another that you'll be honest with them. Instead, simply tell them what you intended to tell them all along.

Dangerous Words

There is another, somewhat related category of words. These are words that aren't evil or useless but can be dangerous. The most dangerous word is Yes.

Yes

Why is "yes" a dangerous word? Isn't "yes" what we want in order to get the next sale, promotion, job, deal? How can "yes" be dangerous when it is exactly what I want? These are great questions.

Our desire to have others agree with us makes the word "yes" very dangerous. "Yes" can have multiple meanings—confirmation, I'm listening to you, permission, and agreement. If someone tells you "yes" and they clearly express one of these meanings, you are OK.

Whew! Red alert canceled.

Where this word becomes dangerous is when you interpret it to mean agreement when in reality no agreement exists. When does this happen?

Imagine someone selling a security system comes to your door. They really want your time, but you're not interested. You tell them you don't have time to talk to them. Naturally, they have been trained to handle this response and ask when would be a good time for them to come back. Perhaps, you say, tomorrow. The sales-person then confirms the time they will return tomorrow, and you say "yes."

In this example, did you really mean it? Will you be waiting with anticipation at your door for this salesperson, or will you plan to be out of the house at that time? You were not committed to the "yes" you gave. It was merely a convenient way to get rid of an inconvenience.

Transpose this situation to a business environment. Many colleagues want to do a good job, and they desire to do good work for any of the possible rewards. They agree to take on a project despite already working far over their own capacity. In order to appear to be a solid team member and worker, they may say yes when they do not have the ability to complete the project.

This appears often in contract work, especially for entrepreneurs who are surviving and desperate. They will say yes to almost any project and timeline, believing that having the work is better than being selective. Unfortunately, this often means they miss the timeline, and the project ends up costing them instead of putting money in their bank account. Worse yet, the relationship with a potential repeat customer is damaged, which reduces the chances of future work and creates more desperation for the entrepreneur.

Imagine the most recent financial crisis. How much would you be willing to bet that in a room full of well-educated and experienced people someone asked the question "Are you sure this (insert new fantastic money-making scheme) is safe (risk-free)? Guess what the response was. Yes. We have seen the results of that catastrophe where many people were convinced to go ahead with high-risk investments, resulting in a near collapse of the financial system.

The word "yes" comes in many forms. You might experience it in some of the following alternate ways. Write down variations you hear in your team environment.

I guess so.	OK.
Sure.	You bet. (This is a favorite where I grew up.)
_____	_____
_____	_____

With luck, most of the situations in which you receive a "yes" do not come with quite so impactful consequences, but it can cause you problems. How do you avoid an empty "yes?"

Create a Culture of No

Obviously, we can't say no to everything, and yes is still a useful word. In order to prevent it from being meaningless, it is important to create an environment where it is accepted and encouraged to have colleagues share contrary opinions, disagree, and tell you "no" if they feel they cannot fulfill your request. "No" is a much more useful word because it typically has fewer meanings. "No" indicates a lack of agreement or refusal.

You may not like to hear "no", but it is a very useful word. When you hear "no", you now know that an avenue of thought or direction is closed to you; you can use your creativity to alter your goals or the means by which you will achieve them. If you are told "yes", when the other person has no intention or unintentionally can't fulfill the request, this is a dangerous position. You may be relying on the actions of this other person---supervisor, colleague, staff member. If they do not follow through, this will have a serious impact on your ability to deliver on your promised outcome. When you hear "no", you can now alter your plan and begin to ask questions that will move you towards problem resolution. Instead of wasting time in limbo, by receiving an empty "yes" you've been given the gift of "no."

Embrace "no" for your team. It is not stimulating obstinacy or whining but encouraging a realistic assessment of abilities and capacity. This increases understanding of the current situation and spurs conversation about the reasons the response was a "no." Is the problem a timeline that is too tight, readjusting priorities, budget restrictions, or restrictive policies of procedures? Knowing the reasons for the "no" can lead to better solutions that will actually be accomplished. The gift of "no" will allow you to achieve much more than living in a world of empty "yes."

Allowing others to start by saying no opens them up to saying yes to what you really need. According to Jim Camp in his book on negotiating, titled *Start With No*, "yes" and "maybe" are not real responses. They create no thinking on the other person's part. When someone says no, however, they begin to think about why they are saying no. Now you are in a position to begin the real conversation.

Activity

This week, record yourself regularly if you can. If this is not possible, pay attention to the phrases you speak. Write down all of the common phrases you use. You may be surprised by how few there are. Now, consider a new or alternative way to respond and try that out for a week. Mix and match to make conversations interesting.

11. Samurai Poker – What Options Do You Have When You Accept Failure?

Warning!

If you are reading this chapter to become a better gambler, I suggest you skip to the next one. Though the title has the word "poker" in it, the content has nothing to do with gambling, reading people, or making a fortune at some lovely green felted table. If that is your intent, I wish you success, but this chapter is about the power of accepting loss in order to gain. The only gambling comes from an experience I had with a philanthropic event that led me to experience the conundrum that when I accepted that I might lose, the opposite happened.

Many years ago, a friend had decided to raise money for the fight against cancer. He and his team were gathering donations to support this charity. They would ride a certain distance and the proceeds would go towards cancer research. He came up with a fun and creative way to encourage people to participate and give. He held a poker tournament.

The entry fee was a $50 donation to the charity. In return, he welcomed all participants to his home where he was hosting a fun poker tournament. No money was used. All entrants played for chips, and prizes were given at the end. Yet, it was this night that would lead to a powerful lesson and much reflection. The night began much as any social evening. Various friends arrived. New acquaintances were made, food was shared, and then the tournament began.

In his living room, he had set up three tables for players. As we sat down, each of us had $50 in chips and play began. It was a fun time, and like many games of this nature, chips changed hands back and forth. Players would gain and give as the night went on and gradually only a few players were left with the chips at each table.

Though I was having fun, at this point in the evening I was ready to go home. I made up my mind to play aggressively as I did not care if I lost my entire earnings to that point. My goal was actually to lose so that I might leave.

Little did I know that, in that moment when I accepted that I could lose everything, I was, instead, on my way to winning more than I ever expected. So, I began to play aggressively. I began betting larger and more on each round. This is when an odd thing started happening. As I became bolder, I began to win more. The other players would often fold, and I would win when I expected to lose.

After a time, I reached a point where I went all in. My partners at the table anted similarly, and playing boldly, I won that hand and the entire table's winnings. Not only had I delayed my goal of finishing and getting home, I had advanced to the final round, where they consolidated the winners of the three tables together to play for the title of champion of the event.

I should note at this time that I am not what you would call a gambler. I do not frequent casinos or host poker nights at my house. I cannot name even one strategy real gamblers use in such a game. As my goal for the evening had not changed, I stuck with the strategy that was working. I was ready to lose all of my chips now, especially as I was at a table with others who had won. I expected the competition to be quite good and probably better than what I would be able to provide.

Play began, and I continued with my aggressive style of play. I would bluff and bid up hands. If the cards were in my favor, I would bid more. My record was not perfect, as I lost many hands, yet my pile of chips grew and grew. Finally, it came down to one hand—all in. It was after midnight and my partners were ready to wrap this up as much as I was.

In the final hand, I was gifted with cards that, in the end, outmatched my opponents. I had done something completely opposite of what I had intended. I WON!

On the way home, I reflected on this situation, as I have many times since. How is it that I won when I set out to lose? How did I become champion when my goal was not to win but to leave?

Perhaps there is an answer in the Bushido code of the samurai of Japan. Samurai are held as a pinnacle of martial warriors. The author of *Hagakure: The Book of the Samurai*, Yamamoto Tsunetomo wrote the following about accepting consequence in order to fulfill duty.

"Rehearse your death every morning and night. Only when you constantly live as though already a corpse (jōjū shinimi) will you be able to find freedom in the martial Way, and fulfill your duties without fault throughout your life."

Certainly, the consequences of winning a fundraiser poker tournament are much lower than contemplating and accepting the loss of your life; however, the concept applies to this situation. Once I let go of my expectations to win, it allowed me to play in a different, more daring way that led to my unexpected victory. What would happen if you could let go of your fear of losing or failing Instead of letting worry dominate you, choose to accept that you may lose or fail. Accepting this gives you options as you may consider choices that you couldn't see or wouldn't contemplate.

What is holding you back right now? Can you accept the consequence if it doesn't work out? Imagine yourself unlimited by stultifying beliefs. What options are available to you? This may feel awkward at first, but practice and see what options it opens for you.

12. Prepare for Constant Change

To improve is to change; to be perfect is to change often.

— *Winston Churchill*

The Golden Formula

People are consistently looking for, not just an answer, but THE answer. There is a desire to reach a pinnacle understanding, process, lifestyle, etc. With this desire comes a matching expectation that, once attained, this state will remain static. This is a large fallacy as life is constantly changing. Further, we had to change to achieve or reach where we are right now. Therefore, we must expect that our circumstances will change again.

There is a reason they call them Golden Ages. It's easy to look back and believe the good times only lasted for a period of time in the past. Given the conditions of the time, the experience may have been positive for those remembering, but conditions don't last. We live in a universe of constant change. Much like a company that rose to prominence on one core product to be overthrown by a startup with a novel idea, the same happens to all those who hang on to the past and hold it up as a paragon of how we should operate, conduct business, or live.

Find what works for you but remember that it will not work forever. At some point, you will need to adapt and change your method slightly or significantly in order to stay on top in your market.

It is a common flaw in human thinking to search for the "Holy Grail", the ultimate solution, the one thing that resolves everything. Time and again, we see this in companies that created something amazing – a product or service – and not long after doing so faded away as what they created becomes irrelevant or is replaced by another company's innovative product or service.

I learned this hard truth on the Ultimate Frisbee field. I remember playing another team and we were pretty evenly matched. They had one great player that countered our overall edge in experience. The other team started strong, and we adjusted our strategy. It worked and we began to win. After the halftime break, we kept to our strategy and suddenly we weren't winning anymore, and we lost the game. After the game, I asked the other captain what happened and he said he could see that we had figured out one of their weaknesses, so he adjusted his strategy. He did, but we didn't, and that is why we lost.

Circumstances are constantly changing, and as leaders we need to adapt. More importantly, we need to create an environment where our teams adapt. Many experts in leadership, who see the increasing pace of change, express the importance of values in an organization, but, most importantly, the value of change. To value change is to create an adaptable, responsive learning organization. It is knowing that in life and business there is no one solution—only the current solution. It is recognizing that there is no great end goal but a constantly moving goal line.

Life all around us adapts. In the movie *Hero With a Thousand Faces*, medical workers respond to the Ebola outbreak in Sierra Leone. The outbreak forced humans to adapt in response to the virus. At the same time, the virus was also experimenting and evolving. Nature is a series of improvements in defense or offense or symbiosis. Business and leadership likewise require constant modification.

The conditions around each moment of time in business are different, much like a snowflake, which forms completely uniquely to the others around it. It is fascinating to consider that each snowflake has a different shape. The conditions around which a snowflake forms are unique to that very location in time. The humidity, temperature, moisture content, wind factor, etc. are not the same across the sky. They vary greatly, thereby causing great variation, in the end, result in a unique snowflake.

How well does your team value change?

What examples do you have that demonstrate how your team or organization has adapted to a problem or change in your industry?

Is each workday relatively the same?

How much are your team members empowered to identify and solve problems?

What processes, procedures, or practices no longer serve the organization and may even be hindering it?

Growth Is NOT Linear

When considering change, it is easy to look at a current fad or experience and try to extrapolate that out. The problem with doing this is that we often extrapolate it as a straight line. Thomas Robert Malthus, a cleric, scholar, and economist, wrote *An Essay on the Principle of Population* in the year 1798. He posited that human population growth is exponential, whereas food production increases are linear. Essentially, he said humans will reproduce faster than we can produce food to feed everyone. As a result, he expected there to be mass starvation and a complete system collapse.

What is the result of this prediction? The human population has not experienced what Malthus predicted. He did not account for advances in technology or global trade. Nor could he foresee population changes as population growth has slowed in many regions. Further, the earth is sustaining more people. How did this happen? Humanity continually adapts. It skews all forecasted lines of growth, development, and disaster.

It's much like how the planets are depicted in orbit around the sun. Every model I have seen places them in a plane of rotation. I trust scientists that this is accurate. What we don't explain well is that our entire solar system is not static in space. It is moving. The sun is moving as we rotate around it. If you truly tracked each planet's movement, it would look more like a spiral than a circle. Similarly, the future is elusive because humanity and world experience move in multiple dimensions all at the same time. We do not sit idly watching world circumstances. We reflect, rally, and respond to them.

I am writing this during the COVID-19 pandemic. This is an amazing example of adaptability. My daughter's friend arranged an online escape room video chat. Companies that provide web communications are making their programs more robust and user-friendly. Though elective surgeries were canceled initially, it was not long before alternate protocols were created to allow them to take place. We have adapted to waiting outside stores to minimize occupancy. We follow the arrows on the floor when shopping for groceries and wear masks wherever we go.

All of these are examples of how we've adapted. If we had not adapted, the Public Health Agency of Canada's model anticipates that 70-80% of our society would be infected with COVID in a short period of time after we first realized its danger. Instead, we have been able to flatten the curve significantly.

Another great example of change involves the development of technology in various countries. The industrial revolution was a powerful change in technology. Many would argue it was a step on the path to the technology we have today. What if you are a country that did not have an industrial revolution? Does that country need to follow that stage of development before they can have phones, computers, and cars? In a linear model, the answer is yes. In reality, the answer is no.

If a country has no wifi infrastructure, they are not going to plan to build a 1G or 2G network when 5G is the latest evolution of the technology. Their advantage is that others have already tested and developed various models. They are able to capitalize on the lessons learned by many other countries that were earlier in the development process. The result is that they can install a wireless telecommunications infrastructure that is better than many countries that started earlier.

There are many examples where growth is not linear

- Moore's law states that the number of transistors in a microchip doubles every two years, and this observation was revised later as processes improved. It now takes only 18 months for the number of transistors on a chip to double.
- Martin Hilbert did his own research showing that information doubles every 3 years and 4 months.
- In the book *Megachange: The World in 2050*, futurists note that information storage grows four times faster than the world economy, and computational power grows nine times faster.
- Consider how fast babies grow into children compared to adult growth over the course of a lifetime. A baby's growth, and therefore human growth, is definitely non-linear.

13. The Learning Process

To thrive in our dynamic world, every leader and every team needs to constantly learn in order to adapt to changes and take advantage of opportunities. Understanding the learning process and committing to our own learning leads the way for our teams and organizations to do the same and thrive.

Four Stages of Competence Model

Developed in the 1970s by Noel Burch, and referenced in many articles, this is a simple model for considering our own development and the development of those we lead. This model can apply to any skill and a person can be at a different level of competency for many different skills.

Unconscious Incompetence

You don't know that you are not competent. You don't know what you don't know.

Conscious Incompetence

You know that you are not competent. This is the most transformational stage, as recognition of a gap in our skill development allows us to proceed to develop that skill.

Conscious Competence

You know that you are competent at a skill. This comes with practice, feedback, and results.

Unconscious Competence

You are practiced to the point that you no longer need to think consciously to execute this skill. The best example is muscle memory.

It is much like driving home from the grocery store. Have you ever arrived home without remembering how you got there? Your mind may have been busy thinking about something else while your body drove you home. You've practiced it multiple times and it didn't require your conscious thought to do it.

This is a great model for understanding the leadership gap. You may have advanced your technical skills as you've advanced in your career. The regular tasks are easy, and you may perform many of them with little mental effort because you are so practiced with them. However, now you've been promoted, and this requires a series of new skills. In some of them, you may feel consciously competent, and in others, you may feel consciously incompetent. It may also be useful to get another person's perspective on your performance to identify areas of development that you didn't realize were needed (unconscious incompetence). Working to increase self-awareness and competence in the skills will make them easier and, with continued practice, allow you to become unconsciously competent and focused on the next skill set you wish to master.

The people you lead are at various stages in this process too. Often frustration arises when you are further along this process in a certain skill than the people you lead. You want them to catch up and perform at your level, but they may not have had the training, practice, or experience yet to achieve this. They may not be aware of their lack of skill and chances are they need your support in improving their level of competence.

Read That Great Book ... Again

Have you read or listened to any outstanding books? Books from which you gleaned a great lesson that helped you to improve a skill or overcome a challenge? Books that gave you insight into yourself, your ways of thinking, or your leadership style?

Leaders are Readers. That is a truth. In today's age, when we have so many modes of learning and resources available to us, I like to say: Leaders Are Learners. Organizations that thrive are learning organizations. Learning organizations are led by leaders who learn.

What are you reading right now? You may have a long list of books you wish to read, and I recommend you get started. The following are some tips on helping you stay accountable for reading all those books on your shelves.

- Set a regular time to read each day. Routine is powerful in achieving goals, and how you dedicate your time determines your priorities. Even if you read for fifteen minutes each day, you will be surprised at how many books you get through in a year.
- Keep a list of books you have read or listened to. This will keep you motivated, and you will be surprised at the end of a year how many books you have read.
- Read for understanding. Consider this your advanced leadership course. Take notes or have a discussion about the content with a trusted mentor, coach, or colleague.
- Join a book club. This will give you structure and a deadline for completing your reading. Further, it will give you an outlet for discussing and thinking about what you've learned. Discussion often deepens and broadens our learning. For extroverts, this can be especially powerful as it allows you to process the information through conversation.

- Start a book club with your team. Consider what book might be useful for your team's growth. You can have members of the team take turns facilitating the discussion. In addition to contributing to your learning, it will also serve as a common team event and strengthen the unity of your team.

At the beginning of this section, I recommended reading a great book you loved one more time. Not everyone likes to reread books. You may think you've absorbed all the relevant information and that reading the book again may not add much to your understanding or perspective on the matter. I know I used to think this way. I used to think there was little point in reading a book again. Since the contents of the book didn't change, I couldn't see a reason to read it again, as this would take time away from reading other books. I was only looking at one side of the relationship with the book.

What I was missing is that the other side of the relationship is me. The book may not change, but I do. When it comes to learning, we connect new experiences to old experiences. Our brain actually builds layers of memory and understanding. What I failed to realize is that as I grow, my context and understanding expands. There may be many concepts I completely missed the first time reading the book because I was not developed enough yet to understand them.

This is why I recommend looking at the best five books you've read over the past decade. Choose one and read it again. Prior to rereading this book, write down what lesson(s) you remember learning from it the first time. As you read the book, or when you finish, write down any new lessons that you learned or relearned from reading it a second time. Consider how your context has changed and how that allows you to learn new lessons from the same material.

Leaders are Readers and Re-readers.

Read to Teach.

Leaders are Learners, and Leaders are Teachers.

Read, listen, and watch content to learn, and take this to the next level by considering how you can use the content to teach your team. Every successful leader considers the development of their team. When you are learning, learn beyond yourself. Learn the material in a way that allows you to teach it to your team. Model learning and teaching for your team, and they are more likely to do this for their teams. This is what creates a culture of learning in the organization. If everyone is learning to teach, it reinforces the value of learning in your organization. It will increase the speed of sharing and thus your ability to adapt to changing circumstances as an organization.

14. What If It's Not About You?

You may worry that someone is going to be angry or disappointed with you, or you may desire to meet their expectations in order to make them happy. Before difficult performance review conversations, I practiced what I would say as I worried about how the other person would react. It took years to realize that how another person thinks, feels, and responds has very little to do with us.

What another person takes from a conversation with you is entirely dependent on their context—their world view. What is their context? It is the sum of experiences and beliefs that shape the way we see the world.

Context is much like the filters used in theater lighting. A filter is a colored transparent sheet of plastic that is placed in front of a light to give off a different color. Place a blue filter in front of a white light, and, voila—the lighting and mood turn blue.

In the filter analogy, we act much like the white light. What we think we are broadcasting is going out to the other person, but what they take in goes through their own filter. As a result, what we thought was white light turns blue when received by the other person. This is similar to messages; the other person will not hear everything you have to say. Their brain is already sorting what is relevant and irrelevant to them, resulting in great potential for misunderstanding. You can share your message, but you can never be sure which parts of the messages are embraced or heard.

Though it can be challenging, there is also great freedom in this. I firmly believe that I can't offend someone else. Certainly, I can say something to which another person may take offense but determining what is offensive is always based on the receiver. Through the receiver's context, they determine if a comment or action is offensive. When a person gets upset, it is not because of what you did. It is because of the messages or beliefs they have about what you said. You may not have said anything you consider offensive, but their filter identified an insult.

Think about a time you had an interaction with someone who seemed unhappy with you. You may have asked them "What is wrong?" or "What did I do?" The other person may expect you to know, but you can't know how they feel and what they are thinking.

When I was in graduate school, I was a residence director. This position is similar to a property manager for university-operated residences. Part of my responsibilities was working with students and resolving conflicts. Misunderstanding or miscommunication was usually the issue, as demonstrated by an incident between two young women. The first woman was upset because the second hadn't said hello to her when they passed on the way to class. She felt snubbed and was angry. Meanwhile, the second knew something was wrong but didn't remember the interaction. She was focused on a test and didn't notice much happening around her that day. This is a great example of how one person took offense. The second woman didn't cause the offense. Instead, the first woman interpreted, through her context, that she should feel offended by the action, and she did.

Consider how knowing this can ease your work. Take some of the responsibility off your shoulders for knowing everything that another person is thinking. Ask for clarification when you observe someone having a strong reaction to what you've shared. Remove a further burden by knowing that you are not responsible for any person's emotions or reactions other than your own.

15. Receiving Feedback and Recognition

If you have earned the respect of those around you, at some point you will most likely be complimented on your performance. For many, this is uncomfortable. Yet it doesn't have to be. When receiving recognition, remember this simple process.

1. Say "Thank You."
2. Reiterate what they said in a way that shows them you heard the recognition given. E.g., "I appreciate your praise for our completion of the Siren Project."
3. Recognize your team. "My team worked hard to make this happen. I am fortunate to lead such a talented group."
4. Remember that as a leader you are receiving praise not only for yourself but for your entire team. You are your team's representative.

Receiving feedback is simpler still.

1. Say "Thank You."
2. Reiterate what they said in a way that shows them you heard the feedback given. E.g., "It sounds like I could have communicated better prior to presenting our report."

3. If you know what you will do in the future, you can share this now. Otherwise, you can let the other person know that you will think about their feedback and get back to them. It's OK to take time to reflect on what was shared with you. It may raise additional questions you want to discuss so that you can do better the next time this situation arises.

CAUTION: Whenever receiving recognition or feedback, never belittle your contributions or disparage yourself. There is no need to do this. Not only does it show a lack of confidence, but it also disrespects the person giving you the feedback or recognition. This person believes you are important enough to take their time to give you special attention in the form of praise or constructive criticism. Respect this by gracious acceptance, knowing that you've earned it.

Section Four – Understanding and Moving Forward

Your life purpose is to use your own personal transformation to help transform society. Once mentored by another, you will now mentor others. — *Unknown*

16. The Myth of Being Self-Made

I enjoy reading biographies and autobiographies as well as listening to interviews with successful people. Though I don't often hear them refer to themselves as self-made men or women, I often hear others refer to them this way. I'm not sure that it is very accurate, though.

What is a self-made person? The phrase indicates that the person has achieved all their accomplishments solely from their own effort. If that were true, we wouldn't need leaders.

In her biography, Kym Gold considers herself a self-made businessperson. For those unfamiliar with her background, she is the co-founder of the designer jeans brand True Religion and has created multiple designer labels in the fashion industry. She is an amazing and interesting business person. Like so many business people, her story involves hard work—a lot of hard work. It is true that she worked exceedingly hard to create her fashion business. However, this was not done one hundred percent on her own. While she was creating the business, she relied on those around her, especially her family, to watch her kids. Self-made is an interesting moniker, but a bit inaccurate. There are always others we rely on to achieve our goals, whether building a business or leading one.

There is a reason so many authors, actors, and people in public positions thank their spouse, parents, and partners. Their success really does hinge on receiving some level of support from others. We get by on our own, but we excel when we work together as a group.

Sarah Blakely, the founder of Spanx, is someone who would be considered "self-made" by many; yet she readily acknowledges that her company never would have started without securing a partnership with a plant to manufacture her product. It in no way diminishes the dogged persistence she showed in visiting various manufacturers and getting turned down repeatedly. Nor does it detract from the countless hours and hands-on approach she put into marketing and selling her product. It's part of the reality of making her vision and product a reality. She needed a manufacturer. She got one and created a billion-dollar business.

Needing others doesn't detract from the hard work that is done as a leader. You're not on this journey alone. There are many who will help you, and you will need a team. That team may include employees, partners, family, childcare workers, restaurants and food providers, internet service providers, city services, etc. To have our greatest impact as a leader requires us to work with and rely on others. Our success depends on it.

17. The Thrive Curve

Having worked with many leaders over the past years, I have observed a common, though not universal, pattern. I like to call it The Thrive Curve.

Stage 1 – Survival Mode

As human beings, we love survivor stories. Reflect on the number of times survival is the focus of a movie, TV show, or book. This theme permeates our media, though you don't need to read an article or watch a video to experience survival mode. Survival is where a lot of leaders start their journey.

What happens in survival mode? Fear is a constant emotion. Will I fail? What if …? What if …? What if …?

Fear is useful and we've evolved to feel fear for very real reasons. Fear focuses our senses. Fear triggers our adrenalin, enhancing our ability to act. Fear is the reason we've lived long enough to have this discussion about fear.

The problem with living in survival mode is that it narrows our vision. Instead of seeing ten options, we will only see one. Instead of seeing the opportunity, we will see the threat. If we are scrambling to meet our goals every month/week/day feeling like we're never making progress, that means we are in survival mode.

Stage 2 – Change and Stabilize

Eventually, living in survival mode gets old. It takes a lot of energy, and it is trying to exist on a roller coaster of emotion from panic to relief, every week if not every day. At some point, you want a change and decide to take action.

To make a change in how we operate we have to change how we think. Most often this comes about through working with a good coach or mentor who broadens your view and helps you focus, away from rooted behavior patterns toward more successful habits of thought and decision. It may also come through taking a course or engaging others in conversation. The core of change comes from a desire for change and committing to learn and apply new modes of thought and action.

Once you have committed to a new or different pattern, it can take time to see the results in your business or team. Like learning a new skill, you need to apply it repeatedly over time to instill it. It may seem chaotic at times, and though change never comes fast enough, continued practice leads to positive results. As you come out of survival mode, your business will too. You will see it begin to stabilize at a higher level. The lessons of the change become standards of practice, and the organization is operating in a new, more successful way.

Stage 3 – Internal Momentum

As you grow, so does your team. As you grow, so does your organization.

When my daughter was learning to skate, a friend told her she had to fall down a thousand times to learn to skate. I don't know that she fell that many times, but I do know it was a lot. She fell and fell and fell. This didn't stop her. She was determined to become a better skater and continued learning and practicing. Gradually she fell less often, and today she doesn't fall at all.

Much like learning to skate, the fun part is when you've come through the difficult transition, and, instead of you pushing for the change, your team initiates it. Having reached a new level of operation, the team has an internal momentum that pushes forward new changes that continue to evolve the organization.

18. Moving from Hustle and Grind to Business Professional

Many who start in business and leadership begin as hustlers. They are reactive to what is happening in their role, with their team, and in their business. Hustlers exist in what I call survival mode.

Survival Mode: when your focus narrows due to fear or stress and you just try to get through the next task, problem, or responsibility. Most often, you are reacting to whatever most recently came across your desk or entered your inbox. In survival mode, you see fewer possibilities, feel higher stress, and get distracted easily. It's easy to overlook written contracts or forego simple email confirmations to assure you and the other person are in agreement. Though it seems easier at the time, it will often turn into a detriment later.

When you are working to survive, you operate in a way that provides very few options. The choices you make are about expediency and what is in front of your right now, instead of thinking into the future. In survival mode, you are thankful to get any work, meet any deadline, or sign any terms even when they might not benefit you. In survival mode, you are at the mercy of the world around you—your clients, your contractors and subcontractors, your staff. Getting out of the hustle means taking control of your work environment.

Step one is to appreciate your own expectations. It is OK for you to expect good work, timely payment, respectful language, mutually negotiated timelines, etc. When you begin to respect yourself, others begin to respect you.

I was working with a young man who was trying to get out of survival mode. When he realized how much he was hustling, he decided to set different standards for himself. As he became more confident, he noticed that more customers and industry partners wanted to work with him. By respecting his own time and values rather than pandering to everyone else's requests, he actually improved his bottom line and, more importantly, the quality of his experience as a businessperson. His motivation increased. His team's belief in him and their mission skyrocketed.

Remember that in every relationship (business to customer, business to business, leader to team member, leader to supervisor, president to CEO, or life partner to life partner, you are allowed to negotiate the agreements you make. When you respect yourself, you set an example for the other person in the relationship. It sets up the relationship as a partnership of equals rather than a master-servant relationship.

Relationship	To what degree do I negotiate for what I need (5) versus automatically giving the other person everything they ask for (1)?	What will I do about this?
	5 4 3 2 1	
	5 4 3 2 1	
	5 4 3 2 1	

Here are some ways to move from a Hustler to a Professional.

- When discussing partnerships or deals, outline what you need and don't be afraid to challenge the other person if a request seems unreasonable or unaligned with your values, needs, or goals.
- When hiring or onboarding new staff, discuss the values of the organization, responsibilities of the position, and expectations for conduct in the work environment. Give them a written copy in advance or as a follow-up to their orientation.
- Instead of consistently keeping information in your head and expecting your team to know what they are supposed to do, document your procedures, critical business processes, and core values.

Setting down in print how your team will operate may seem constraining. In fact, it is exactly the opposite. It allows your team to know what is expected of them. It brings clarity that allows them to operate at a higher level because they are not confused about where the boundaries are. Jocko Willink & Leif Babin, in their book *Extreme Ownership*, do a great job of outlining this principle. As Special Operations Forces soldiers, they required their team to follow set procedures for as many tasks as possible. Instead of stymying the team, it helped them reserve their mental power for responding to ever-changing situations in combat. If Navy Seals outline their processes in order to improve their chances for survival, what can the same discipline do for you and your team?

If it helps, you can think about the difference between Survival Mode/Hustling and Professional Businessperson in this way. When you are in survival mode you are focused on you. There is a great sense of relief when the next paycheck comes in or the next contract gets signed. It is a personal sense of comfort. On the other hand, moving to a Professional Businessperson involves thinking about your team and setting them up for success. Providing them the guidelines for how you expect them to operate allows them to perform at a high level. As you model working professional habits of operation, so too will your team, allowing everyone to move out of survival mode and create the high-level professional environment that leads to greater success.

Possibility Thinking

I am always amazed when colleagues share that they feel they have no power to make a change, implement a program, or have a meaningful impact without the approval of their leader or senior leader. This is an easy excuse and I understand that in some organizations top-down management means micromanagement, which means all decisions are going through one person. However, there is always a choice. Opportunity exists, and where there is scarcity (for example, of decision-making power), there is also creative potential to operate in a new way. It doesn't always require more money or time, but it does require a different way of thinking about the problem. It requires possibility thinking.

It starts when you realize that everything we have today is a result of challenging the conventional thinking of the time. Why would I use a bow when I have spears? Why would I want a car when I've got a horse? Why would I need a telephone when I can write letters? Why would people want personal computers when we have mainframes?

Consider almost any innovation or creation—a majority of people probably thought it was a stupid idea. They didn't have the skill of possibility thinking and therefore they couldn't imagine that a new creation would be desirable. Yet, after something useful and new is created the nay-sayers take it up and begin to use it much like the rest of the community.

It's important to note that great things don't just happen. It takes consistent, persistent effort. We don't find innovation, we create it. The good news is that there are endless opportunities. Where do you look to find them? The Obstacle Garden.

The Obstacle Garden is a term used to refer to all of the potential problems, pitfalls, challenges, complications, issues, snags, hitches, drawbacks, troubles, worries, hurdles, hiccups, setbacks, and difficulties that you or people you know are facing. Where there is a problem, there is opportunity.

Where There is a Problem There is Opportunity

As a leader, it is important to look for what is possible. I'm not saying you can ignore the current situation around you. But your team will often be focused on this, and they need you to look for the possibility in every decision, initiative, change, and challenge. Each new circumstance may be seen as an obstacle, but it also has potential. Possibility Thinking is a great way to consider how changes in your business and work environment can work toward your benefit and that of your clients, customers, and team.

Profit Is in the Problem

Another way to look at this is that each problem is an opportunity for profit. When circumstances are going well, others don't need us. It is when they have a problem that we can profit from helping to fix it for them.

Some teams focus on the problems and wish they would go away. They don't realize that the profit that fuels the business is generated from problems. As you are able to solve more or bigger problems, you increase your earning potential.

What recent change is your team finding challenging?

_____
_____
_____

What possibility now exists due to the change?

_____
_____
_____

How will I communicate this possibility to my team?

_____
_____
_____

19. See Yourself Beyond Where You Currently Are

You may reach a point in your development, or the development of your team or business, where you feel that you've plateaued. If you feel this way, you have plateaued.

Once you have reached a certain level of revenue, achievement, or whatever metric you like to use, you will stay at this level until you are able to conceive of a higher and greater view of yourself and your organization.

I was working with a client who was struggling to get past $60,000 a month in revenue. Month after month, this was the threshold for his company. Though he desired and saw the potential for greater profit in the company, he couldn't get past this current amount.

To help him, we talked about where he sees the company in the future. How large will it be? How much revenue will it produce? How many people will it employ?

Once we had developed this, it was important for him to realize he is the CEO of this company ... right now. It's not about wanting to be the CEO of a company that size. He is the CEO of a $5 million revenue company. It just isn't built to that size yet.

Knowing this changed the way he saw himself, his team, and his entire operation. In a short time, the company revenue increased to $100,000 a month and continued trending in the right direction. He hired additional staff to handle the expansion of work. He began to see himself as the CEO of the company he will build, rather than seeing himself scrambling to maintain the company that he had.

Don't see yourself as your job right now. Don't see yourself as the leader you are right now at your position. See yourself at the highest level you want to attain. This will prepare you for it and move you toward that goal much faster.

20. As You Change, the World Around You Changes

The power to change the world really does begin with us. Each person is like an atom of water in a pond connected to every other atom of water. What happens to one small droplet has an impact on the droplet of water next to it. It is all connected. That is why webs are such powerful metaphors. When one part of the web is touched, it sends vibrations through the entire web.

Our lives as leaders are very much like this. As we change ourselves, it changes our interactions. Changes to our interactions lead to changes in how others respond to us. It has to, because of how we are connected. This is why it is so powerful to begin by changing ourselves. As we move, we move the world.

I was working with one of my clients and we focused a lot on communication. He wanted to communicate more effectively in the workplace, but he was avoiding talking about what really needed discussing. As we explored this, we were able to reset his belief in communication and to disconnect from the other person's emotion. This greatly helped him to raise important questions. He noticed that he was consistently bringing less tension to meetings, and his team was responding in kind. They told him they noticed how he had changed in a positive way. They were unsure exactly what had changed, yet they recognized it was a good change.

The best part of this situation was not the positive improvement with the team. In fact, the biggest change didn't happen at the office. It was at home. He had been having some difficulty with his son. They were often fighting, and this created a lot of stress. He began practicing the same communication techniques at home, and the relationship with his son improved dramatically. In a short period of time, they were no longer fighting, and he could diffuse tense situations before they escalated. This has led to a high-quality relationship with his son, who now sees his father as a role model he would like to emulate.

This is a terrific example that we are whole beings. Though we often segregate what we are learning for work or business with family life, we don't learn and grow in isolated ways. When we learn, it applies to our entire life. We grow and those around us have to respond. The people in our life are all part of our web. When we vibrate differently on that web, they have to respond differently. Thus, real change starts with us but has an impact far beyond our own life.

Section Five – Skills: Act Like a Leader

In 2019, LinkedIn surveyed over 2000 professionals, asking them what they "want most in a manager." The top five characteristics were about decision-making and caring.

> Problem-solving (68%) was followed by a manager who can manage time effectively (44%), who's decisive (41%), and who has empathy (38%) and compassion (36%).

This section of the book is filled with tips, tricks, and skills that will allow you to give your team what they want so that you can get what you want from them.

THE CORE SKILLS. MASTER THESE AND YOUR LIFE AS A LEADER GETS EASIER.

21. Clarity

Leadership seems hard to a lot of people, and it really can be. Though as a species we have lived millennia on this planet, we still haven't universally figured out how to lead, grow, and get the best from others. Though we get our hair color, height, and biological sex from our genetics, leadership is a social skill that must be observed, taught, and learned. This is why there are so many books on leadership.

Does it have to be this hard, though? Are there any universal truths for working with other human beings to accomplish common goals?

I think there are. It all comes back to relationships, communication, and clarity. When people are clear about what they are supposed to do or achieve, and they have developed the relationships needed to make it happen, it seems almost magical what is accomplished.

How do you arrive at clarity though? Four skills, if practiced, will allow any leader to bring more clarity to their work and gain better results from their team. Learn how to Ask, Listen, Acknowledge, and Decide.

The first two activities are equally important and can happen in either order, depending on the situation. Sometimes a colleague will come to you with a question, and you will start by listening. Other times you may initiate the questions and then listen intently to what the person is sharing with you. Practicing both will get you the information you and your team need to know to make your best possible decisions.

The skills for clarity are Ask, Listen, Acknowledge, and Decide. Where some may think that decision-making consumes the most time, it is really the first two activities of Asking and Listening that take the majority of our efforts. Acknowledging others takes very little time. Thus, when the first three activities are practiced, decision-making requires much less time and can be done with a greater degree of confidence. Spend a majority of your time on the first two activities and the rest gets much easier.

22. Ask

Do you know how the water comes out of your tap? Do you know how the water got to your house? Do you understand the process of purifying it to make it drinkable?

Most of us have no idea exactly how this process works, but we surely appreciate this bit of modern magic, and we definitely understand how it impacts our lives.

As a leader, our role is much like the person who turns on that tap. We don't have to have the answers, but it is up to us to ask them.

If you or your team are unclear about a project, decision, or task, it is most likely that you haven't asked and answered the question you need to be answered. Confusion is often the result of unasked and unanswered questions. When I am unsure of how to proceed, I ask, "What question do I need answered in order to make this decision?" This helps me clarify what I need to know in order to feel ready to respond. At times I have the answer, and asking the question provides clarity and reinforces my decision. Other times I determine a course of action to get the answer so that I can be in a better position to decide.

Many people have the misperception that it is a leader's responsibility to know. They expect a leader to know what to do, what the "right" decision is, how to proceed, solve a problem, or provide a miracle. Experience shows that no one has an internal tome of universal answers. No leader who achieved great things knew exactly how to get there. No one made progress without making mistakes.

Yes, a leader can decide what to do next, and making better decisions often involves including others in the process. Yet, some of the best ideas come when someone chooses to ask a question, raises a possibility, notes a problem, or requests clarity.

As human beings, we want to feel that we have control in our lives. For many, they believe if they are talking, they control the conversation, when in fact it is the person asking questions that has control. They are guiding the conversation and gaining valuable information based on their goals for the conversation.

Asking questions is also a great way to show our interest in the other person. There is an inherent desire in our being that wants to share what we do, what we've learned, our ideas, experience, and knowledge. When in doubt, ask. Many people fear that this will upset the person they are asking. They don't realize that most of the time, the other person is more than willing to share information with them. In fact, I am no longer surprised by the response I get when asking others about themselves. Everyone wants to be understood, and asking questions about them improves their connection with you. It demonstrates your interest in who they are, not merely what they can do for you. It can take more time, but asking questions will get you the support and cooperation you seek much faster than most other means.

Asking Serves Others

Having facilitated groups for years, I like to tell attendees to ask any and all questions they may have. If they feel hesitant, I ask them to still ask their questions in order to serve the others in the group. We often forget that we are not the only one in the room with that question. Sometimes colleagues hold back, worrying about what the others on the team will think. I can answer that question right now— RELIEF! Too many times, a question goes unasked when the majority of the group wants the answer to it. When you ask a question, it serves everyone. It puts the topic into a conversation, which gives everyone permission to discuss it. Now that it is present in the conversation, solutions, opportunities, and contingencies can all be planned.

You don't know what you don't know, and that is OK.

Knowing that there are many areas of knowledge of which you are ignorant is a great benefit. It allows you to ask the questions that need to be asked.

Whenever we hired a company to build a new residence for us, I always had one question I would ask during planning meetings. "What have I not asked that I should have?" or "What question do you usually get asked that I haven't asked yet?" I told the contractor, "I don't know what I don't know." Asking questions this way uses the contractor's expertise to limit my ignorance and reduce risk in the project.

Problem? Ask the Right Question.

If you are struggling with an issue and seem to have no resolution, it is probably because you haven't asked the question that you need answered. Questions are how we engage our mind to solve problems. What stymies the creative process is much more likely to be a lack of good questions rather than an abundance of information. If you are struggling with a situation, consider:

What question has not been asked yet?

What question, if answered, would allow me to make a decision and move forward?

Have I given my team an opportunity to ask questions or brainstorm what questions to ask that will create a higher level of assurance for making a decision?

It's easy to forget that seeking the answer is all about asking questions. When you feel too focused on the result, come back to asking questions. You might reach your desired result, but you might surprise yourself and attain something better.

How to Ask Good Questions

If you practice using three key words, you will automatically improve the questions you are asking—what, who, and when.

What is simple. What are we going to do? It doesn't get much simpler.

Who is vital? Without a name attached to the What, nothing will get done. There must be someone responsible even if multiple people will be helping with the project.

When is the engine? So many professionals forget to place a deadline on when they need a response or result. When we have a date, this becomes the engine that drives our efforts forward.

C. Northcote Parkinson long ago introduced the theory that tasks will expand to fill the time allotted them. Though he published a number of management principles, this one became so popular it is now called Parkinson's law. It is commonly referred to when demonstrating the importance of deadlines for completing tasks.

"When" gives a deadline, and people work well when they know their deadline. Without it, there is no impetus pushing the project forward; it gets lost among other priorities that do have deadlines.

Sit with the Silence

The last step in asking really great questions is to allow the silence to happen after you ask them. This silence gives the team time to think, if they need to, about what has been proposed. When seeking volunteers for assignments, it creates a bit of discomfort, which encourages them to volunteer. It also communicates that you are not taking on this task, which is perfectly acceptable if it is better accomplished by your team. You are a leader and have other responsibilities.

Paint the Elephant in the Room to Reduce Misunderstanding and Missed Information

There is a commonly used expression that I heard growing up in

North America that refers to a situation where there is an unspoken topic that everyone knows, but no one is willing to bring up in conversation—the elephant in the room. I always thought it was a little strange as the only elephants in North America are in zoos or circuses, but I can understand the meaning of this phrase. After all, elephants are huge! If you were in a room with one, it would be odd for no one to mention it.

Let's replace the elephant with any topic that makes us uncomfortable. Why does it make us uncomfortable? We anticipate the emotional reaction of the person receiving our idea or comment, and we worry that it will be negative. Our emotions may increase our anxiety and encourage us to put off raising an important question due to possible unwanted reactions. If we can recognize our own emotions and put them aside, it allows us to ask uncomfortable questions without emotionally charging them. The more we are able to remove our emotion from the topic, the easier our conversations become, creating a culture of open communication.

When you remove your own emotion and ask the questions that address everyone's discomfort or confusion, you benefit the group. They will appreciate someone bringing up the undesirable topic, especially if it is you, the leader. When you mention the unmentionable, it gives the entire team permission to discuss it. When you come to the conversation without energetic emotion, you set the tone for an open discussion about this important topic.

It's like an invisible elephant sitting in the meeting room with you and your team. Though no one can see it, everyone can feel it. It is an intangible known quantity. If the elephant is a problem and you can't see it because it stays invisible, you will get stepped on by the elephant. If you paint the elephant, you can move out of the way when it steps. When you see the problem and you are able to discuss it, you will find the solutions you need to solve it. Once you ask a question directed at the issue, it's like painting that invisible elephant. Now everyone can see it and all can discuss it. There is permission to address it.

Priya Parker, an expert in meeting facilitation, notes that meetings don't usually suffer from unhealthy conflict but from unhealthy peace. This means the group is ignoring what is needed to discuss in order to avoid uncomfortable feelings. Yet, if you don't discuss that elephant in the room, it's likely to stomp on you.

Often it is the subject no one wants to talk about that is the most important to discuss. In fact, discussing it often leads to opportunities instead of further problems. When the elephant stays invisible, the problem persists. Worse, it grows. That's right, the elephant gets bigger, which makes it more mentally difficult to address.

Consider what topics you or your team have avoided. Clear your next agenda and make them the sole and total focus of your conversations. How will you feel when this is done? How good will it be for your team to have shared their thoughts regarding the problem or topic?

Activity

What questions have you not raised in a meeting because you feel uncomfortable with the topic or the possible response you might receive from your team?

_____
_____
_____
_____
_____

What are you feeling when you think about these topics?

_____
_____
_____
_____
_____

Being aware of your reaction, how can you prepare to appear calm when raising this discussion with your team?

_____
_____
_____
_____
_____

23. Listen

Growing up, I was a fan of superheroes. They had amazing powers and saved the world. What could be cooler than that?

I thought it might be awesome to be a superhero myself. As I got older, I realized that I couldn't see through walls, stop a speeding locomotive, or fly through the air. Though I didn't find these powers, my search led me to realize a very human superpower that we all have access to, and that is listening.

Nothing in the world connects two people like listening fully and intently. Truly listening to someone creates trust and allows them to open up, share, and feel heard. If you provide this for another person, they will feel a strong connection to you.

When we listen and use the simple technique of mirroring back to the other person what they have said, it shows them we are listening, and it calms them. This is observable in confrontation. When one person is upset, how the other person responds will fuel the anger or disrupt it. Getting angry in response to an upset person will increase their anger. Conversely, remaining calm and using listening techniques like mirroring most often calms the other person, which allowed us to work together more effectively to solve the concern.

Your role when listening is not to say the right thing or have the right answer. The person speaking has their own answers. Your job is to act as a mirror reflecting back to them what they are saying. Often by speaking with you they will hear their own solutions.

I remember a keynote I listened to a long time ago. He was a former school counselor. One day a young person came to him. She was upset and needed to talk. She came into his office, sat down, and proceeded to vent what she was feeling. At the end of the session, she thanked him for helping her solve her problem and told him his advice was terrific. The funny inconsistency is that he never gave her any advice. In fact, other than the occasional vocable to show he was listening, he didn't speak any words. This young person did _all_ the talking. She needed someone to listen to her so that she could process what she was feeling and thinking. Having someone else listen allowed her to hear herself and create her own resolution.

You have this power for the people with whom you work. Sometimes we get so focused on the end product that we forget there are often wonderful solutions that come up in the process. Listening brings forth brilliance. It is a valuable skill as it helps others on your team think. It is a way of assisting others in ordering and processing the intangible thoughts in their minds into clear and concrete ideas and actions. It is a way to help them gain clarity. Once your team has clarity, they will be a mighty force. Listening creates clarity which leads to powerful action.

Listening Takes More than Two Ears

There is an old saying that we have two ears and one mouth, so we should listen twice as much as we speak. I can appreciate the sentiment, but the adage is too simple. We use much more than our two ears when we listen. Our ears can only hear sounds. This allows us to register the words a person shares, but there is more to listening. If we only use our ears, we can hear another person without truly listening to them.

If merely hearing someone speak does not indicate we are listening, then what is listening? Listening is a full-body pursuit. In addition to our ears, we use our eyes to pick up on nonverbal and physical cues that give context and reveal hidden meaning. The olfactory in our nose receives information via pheromones and subtleties of scent that may not even register consciously, yet still impact our assessment of the conversation. Our body shows that we are attentive, offering encouragement and demonstrating support. All the while, our mind is churning, processing all of this information, analyzing what is being said, and considering how to respond. Listening well requires all of our senses and our mind operating in a highly focused capacity to observe and understand another person.

In many cultures, elders are a great example of people with practiced listening skills. They fill the role of mentors and advisors, using patience, observation, and their honed listening skills to reflect, paraphrase, and ask questions that get to the heart of the matter in minutes, when your friend listened for hours without ever touching on what the core issue was.

Chris Voss, a former hostage negotiator for the FBI, says that listening is the most intense activity a person can do. It doesn't matter if the conversation is a hostage negotiation or a weekly one-on-one meeting with a team member. Listening takes focus, attention, and energy in order to truly understand and help the other person.

Asking Allows the Other Person to Feel Heard

In my previous career as well as serving in various community organizations, I have had the blessing of interacting with people in a variety of emotional states. Dealing with happy people is pretty easy, so let's discuss the opposite side of the spectrum—angry people.

I firmly believe that one of the strongest desires we have as humans is to be heard. If you review significant moments in history such as teacher strikes in Canada, student protests in China's Tiananmen Square, the Arab Spring, or the reaction to George Floyd's death in the United States, there is a recurring theme. The theme carries across music, film, literature, art, and other media in our cultures. That theme and desire are to be heard and recognized. As a result, the fastest way to upset people is to ignore them. A consistent source of conflict isn't disagreement of opinion. Often it is the lack of acknowledgment of what a person has said. Knowing this, we can do the exact opposite to create a better outcome for us and the other person in conversation. When the other person feels heard, their defenses drop and we can productively discuss what is important.

he First Response Is the Worst Response

It can create nervousness when there is a seemingly difficult issue to discuss. You might feel anxious about the other person's response to what you are going to share. This is natural and common. That is why I want you to remember that:

> The first response is the worst response.

The first time a person hears information that they find challenging, they go into a completely different state of mind. It is almost like they transform into a different person because the information is out of alignment with their thoughts, beliefs, or desires. It may be a surprise to them, and they react by going into a defensive mode. In this state, there is little to no possibility of productive conversation. It is often best to give them time and space to reflect on what was communicated. When you discuss it with them again, they will be less emotional about it and you can talk about it constructively.

Knowing how emotional people can get, understand that the first conversation is rarely the last conversation. Don't waste energy trying to convince, explain, or justify if you are receiving a strong response from someone. They are not hearing you. Repeat. They are not hearing you. They have gone into a protective place in their mind. Their defenses are up and you are the enemy (so to speak).

One way to counteract this is to listen. Listening allows them to expel some of their energy. It allows them to feel heard and that will help to calm them down.

Another way is to give them some time to sit with the idea or feedback you provided. It doesn't always need to be a long time, and discussing the issue gets easier. It is no longer a surprise. They have come out of survival mode and are able to discuss the topic.

I remember when I was a Resident Advisor in college. For those unfamiliar with the title, it's the leader of a floor of students living in a dormitory, or what is more commonly called a residence hall. I was responsible for creating a sense of community and enforcing the rules.

Our campus was what you call a "dry" campus, which means that alcohol consumption was not allowed on the premises, regardless if you were of legal age to drink alcohol. One night, I was visiting one of my floormates when I noticed alcohol in his room. As this was against the rules, I documented the situation, which resulted in disciplinary action for him. He was livid and had a few colorful names to call me. His first response was pretty bad.

It wasn't a week later that he saw me as we passed each other on campus and he stopped me purposefully to let me know that he wasn't angry, and he apologized for what he had said. We were OK after that. His first response was the worst response.

Replace '"We" with "I"

Have you ever talked with someone who speaks as though everyone around them thinks the same way? We like the vending machine where it is. Everyone is upset about the new policy. All of us think this idea is crazy.

Speaking in generalizations is a method to avoid accountability for our thoughts, actions, and opinions. It doesn't tell us much about what other people think, but it gives us insight into how the person who's generalizing thinks.

The language others use tells you a lot about them, and here is the universal translator. Replace the words "we" or "everyone" with the word "I."

When someone uses an absolute or general phrase, they are trying to hide behind a collective anonymity. Unknowingly, they are telling you exactly what they think, not what the majority thinks. When you replace any all-encompassing word (e.g., we) with "I", you begin to understand what the other person thinks. When they make a statement, they are really telling you their opinion. After all, how do they know what everyone thinks? They don't. However, with a simple word substitution, you can very easily determine what that person thinks, because they just told you.

24. Acknowledge

Acknowledging another person is very powerful. The most powerful example of this is between a parent and child. When you tell your child you love them, it acknowledges their special relationship with you. It communicates that you see them and appreciate them in your life.

Invisibility is not restricted to a cloak that Harry Potter wears. Many people feel invisible in their everyday lives. Perhaps you feel invisible from time to time.

Acknowledgment is an impactful way of telling someone you see them and they have value.

I remember Than, who used to clean the floors in our building. Every day, dozens of people would walk by him, caught up in their work, lives, or discussing the new show on Netflix. Nobody ever stopped to talk to Than until one day Sarah did. She didn't stop long. In fact, it was less than a minute. What she said wasn't complicated. She used simple words. "Hi. I'm Sarah. I want to thank you for cleaning the floors out here. They look great."

This one, seemingly small, interaction confirmed for Than that he is a person and a person of worth. It was a minor interaction for Sarah, but can you guess whose floors always got cleaned the best after that?

It doesn't take long to acknowledge others. As a leader, dedicate time towards this.

My colleague, Clint, demonstrated this well. He worked in student housing. His primary job was managing a residence full of university students. He set aside time intentionally to acknowledge students who were contributing in positive ways. It always made him laugh how initially they thought they were in trouble. He could see the concern on their faces. When he then acknowledged and praised the great work they were doing, the students' faces lit up and both he and the students left feeling great. Guess how long these meetings were—five minutes. He treated these meetings with the same importance as any meeting he had, and it made a difference. It reinforced the behaviors and attitudes valued in the residence, and it brightened both their days.

Where I grew up, everyone acknowledged each other. Though I grew up in a small town, I didn't know everyone. Yet, wherever I went I would receive a smile and a nod or a wave. It might be through a windshield or passing someone on the street or in the store. It didn't matter. I was always acknowledged. Seeing the people in the community acknowledge one another created a community of caring. No one was invisible, and a seemingly small act created a strong sense of community.

Consider who could use some acknowledgment in your organization.

Activity

Take a walk around a mall, campus, downtown core, or well-used park. Observe what people are doing. Who is acknowledged by others? Who is overlooked or unnoticed? How are people acknowledging each other?

In your workplace, business site, or community space, take note of those you see and practice acknowledging them by simply saying hello or thanks.

Acknowledge your leader or a peer in your organization. (It may surprise you to learn that your leaders and senior leaders don't receive praise often, even if they are doing a great job). Consider doing this in person or sending an anonymous thank you card.

Ask the leader of your organization to attend one of your meetings to praise your team.

25. Decide

The next section will go into further depth on this topic. This step is last because if you have asked good questions, listened closely to the responses, and acknowledged your team's thoughts, a decision often presents itself or you have enough information to make a more informed decision. Don't be afraid to make a decision. Understand that it is one of many. It's like picking out a grain of sand in the desert. There are an infinite number of granules left to find.

DECISION MAKING

I am not a product of my circumstances. I am a product of my decisions.

— *Stephen Covey*

26. Making Decisions – The Infinity of Every Decision

Think about the many decisions you make in a day. What time should I wake up? Do I eat breakfast or not? What do I eat for breakfast? What should I wear? What time do I leave the house? How early do I want to join the web meeting? All of these decisions can occur in only the first few minutes you are awake.

Think about when you arrive at your company. What decisions face you now? What do I need to prepare for the first meeting? How will

I handle the HR issue? Who do I need to follow up with on the project? When can I put together that report? What goes into the report?

Many people get caught up in making one decision as though that decision is a period at the end of a sentence when in reality it is a continuation in an infinite stream of decisions. Each decision is relevant for the time in which it was made, but like bread, it has a shelf life and gets stale and moldy over time. Think back on a small or broad part of your life. You made a series of decisions. If you had stopped making decisions at any point in that period, your life would have stopped. Each decision took you in a direction towards the next decision.

The good news is that if there is an infinite chain of decisions we make, it lessens the expectation we put on each decision. If we make choices that turn out negative, we can make new choices that may result in more positive outcomes. Forgetting this, you can get stuck in the paralysis of fearing to make the "right decision."

I want to make your life easier right now by telling you that there is no such thing as a right decision. I believe that so strongly I will repeat it. There is no such thing as a right decision. There are only decisions and consequences, which lead to more decisions. Accepting this principle will allow you to make more decisions in your life and keep you from getting stuck in indecision.

Many people worry about making the "right" decision. A lot of pressure is put on the choice you will make, which makes it more difficult to decide. In school, we are taught how not to make mistakes. For many, the lesson becomes deeply anchored in an emotional fear of making mistakes. This too adds pressure to the decision-making process. Not wanting to make a mistake leads to a very powerful result—making no decision.

Delaying decision making because of fear has severe consequences. It creates a lot of stress in the decision-maker. It also has a terrible impact on the team. It holds them back from accomplishing their work and they may come to doubt your ability as a leader.

Early in my former career, Seymour Schulich, a Canadian businessman with ownership in a number of different resources and other companies, was giving a talk at the university that left me with one great piece of wisdom regarding decision making. He talked about his partners and how together they looked back on all the decisions they had made that led to the creation of a billion-dollar company. Over ten years, they found they were right 3 out of 10 times. The most important lesson was that they made decisions and continued to make decisions. If a group of dedicated individuals can create a billion-dollar company being right 30% of the time, imagine what you can do.

Decide When to Decide

It is better to decide and make a mistake than to not decide and, through indecision, allow confusion and inaction. You don't have to be hasty, and there is a simple method to help you move forward in your decision making.

Set a deadline for when you will make your decision!

It is really that simple. Having a deadline for when you will make the decision will focus your thought. Have you ever noticed how much gets accomplished when there is a deadline? Without a timeline, it is easy to worry, ponder, and delay. This doesn't help our decision making, but it certainly adds to our stress. Setting a deadline forces you to make a decision and serves you and those you lead. It forces you to make a decision, and that helps you practice the skill of making decisions. The more you practice it, the better you get.

Setting a deadline also helps your team. It communicates to them that you are reflecting on the decision. It also helps them feel that the issue, idea, or question is being considered and moving forward. You haven't made the decision yet, but you have done something. Your team will appreciate knowing when you will make a decision so that they can plan accordingly. If you leave a decision in limbo, your entire team stays in limbo. This is the most uncomfortable position to be in—not knowing.

Some people think the most difficult circumstance is hearing bad news. Instead, it is the stagnation of indecision that is the hardest situation. Upon hearing bad news, you can make choices, consider options, and act. A lack of decision is paralyzing and halts progress. It creates many negative emotions such as frustration, anger, and fear.

Consider a time you had to make a tough decision. Maybe you had to decide:

- Will I leave my current job for a new job?
- Do I end a significant relationship?
- Should I discipline or fire an employee?

If you felt conflict and stress trying to decide what to do, then you understand the difficulty of indecision. Straddling a fence is more painful than standing in front of it or climbing to the other side. Decisions affect us similarly. It is painful to worry, fret, and overanalyze. On the other hand, it is freeing to decide because now all of your energies can focus on the next steps. Giving or receiving bad news is never fun, but it lets you know where you stand and allows you to move forward.

No One Chooses the Poorer Decision

When weighing options, are you going to choose what appears to be the worst option? Excepting self-destructive behaviors, you are most likely going to choose the best decision available to you.

This is important to keep in mind when evaluating others' choices. Your team will need to make decisions; and, like you, they will be making the best decision they can, given the information they have at that time. Can anyone do better than that?

Also consider that no matter how much planning, analysis, and debate go into preparing to make a decision, you still do not control the outcome. You cannot know what the result will be. Therefore, you are consistently required to make decisions without knowing the outcome with certainty.

This is why learning is so important. Reflect on the decisions you and your team make in order to learn why and how you made them. This will make you all better decision-makers in the future. No one is infallible, and you are bound to make mistakes, as will your team. Reflecting on mistakes and the decisions that led to them will improve team decision making, thereby improving performance and adaptability to changing circumstances.

Activity

Consider a recent decision you or your team made that had a positive or negative result. (It is useful to look at decision making that results in positive results as well as when the results aren't what we desire.)

How did you come to make that decision? What was your process? What assumptions, facts, or information influenced your decision?

Would you make this decision if placed in similar circumstances again? Would you use the same decision-making process? If not, what would you change to feel more confident in the decision?

Individual versus Group Decision Making

There is a lot of research on decision making. If I were to sum it up, there are a couple of foundations to remember when trying to decide whether it is best to consult a group or have an individual make the decision.

Group Decision Making

Involving a group in decision making works best when you have time. A group will bring diversity of thought to the problem or question and can provide more robust problem solving. Further, by engaging a group in this process you increase engagement in the final solution.

Individual Decision Making

In times of emergency, when little time is available to make a decision, seeking the counsel of a committee can be disastrous. This is why emergency services use the Incident Command System—a system with a hierarchy for decision making and command and control. It delineates individual decision-making authority to create a clear direction and response to an emergency.

In your organization, there will be times when you may need to make decisions without the ability to consult the team in advance. The timeline may be too tight. In this case, it is important for the decision-making authority to be clear.

To achieve this, it is important to build credibility and trust with your team. If you've involved them in other decisions, you've demonstrated your trust in them. This trust will be returned in times when you are not able to involve them in decisions requiring immediate attention.

27. Manage the Gray

When I was a young professional, I took every opportunity I had to ask experienced leaders about leadership. Often it was the same question, "What have you noticed that makes leaders successful?" I received varied answers, but there is one that will always stick out in my mind.

I was interviewing the Director of Student Housing at the University of North Carolina. This position is responsible for over 8,000 students housed in 40 different buildings. It takes a large team to clean, maintain, and provide programming for this size operation, and the director had hundreds in his employ. I asked him what he looks for in a good leader, and his answer surprised and amazed me. Reflecting on my experience over the years of leading others since that time I have come to understand what he meant.

He told me that there are lots of good people and decent leaders, but what really separates the great from the merely good is the ability to Manage the Gray. At work, there are many tasks and decisions that seem black and white or have a somewhat simple solution. Many people can handle these, but it is when the questions are tougher and have no clear answer that leaders are truly tested. This gray area of uncertainty is where leadership is needed most. How a person navigates the unknown shows their ability to truly lead.

Managing the Gray is a skill and one that you can practice. Here is one tool to help you develop your ability to manage uncertain situations.

Find an article in your field or ask a colleague about a difficult situation they've dealt with somewhat recently. Get the details while intentionally not learning how they handled the situation. Next, set aside some time to review the facts of the situation. Think about all of the questions you want to ask to learn more about what is happening.

- What could be done to prevent this?
- What communication is needed? To whom? When?
- What resources are available?
- What is my timeframe for making decisions?
- What is the impact on the organization or its reputation if we … do nothing? React in a specific way?

Afterward, discuss with your colleague how they handled the situation and compare to your insights on how you would have handled it. Case studies are a great way to develop the skill of Managing the Gray.

28. Living in a World Where You Don't Have to Be Right

In many conversations, there is a felt need to prove that you are right. There is a desire to have the other person agree to what you are saying and a belief that if you talk enough, persuasively enough, using the perfect words, tone, and body language, that you will get them to see that you are right. Unfortunately, this is the least likely way to convince someone you are right. Moreover, it misses the greater point, that "rightness" is a distraction if communication is what you are truly hoping to achieve.

If you are striving to be "right," it means you are not listening. You may think you are convincing the other person, but you are really only convincing yourself. Think back to a time that you felt someone was trying to convince you they were "right." How did this feel? How did you respond? Were you convinced they were "right?"

Being "right" is simply holding on to an opinion. You don't convince people by telling them they are wrong, yet you *can* influence others by acknowledging how they feel and asking them questions. It's not your job to agree or get others to agree with you. Your talent comes into play in creating useful conversation. Understand the other person's perspective and they may come to believe in yours.

29. Deal With the Big Stuff

I was talking to my colleague, Gord, one day. He is a fellow coach who specializes in sales skills and development. He mentioned the importance of dealing with the big stuff and not the chicken shit stuff when you are a leader.

I thought this was a great way to simplify a very common problem. Often when there is a problem that seems too big, or we do not know how to handle it, it's easier to ignore or avoid it. This is a natural response to stressors, though not a useful one in the long-term for your organization, team, or yourself.

Consider right now what the biggest issue, challenge, or opportunity is that you have in front of you. What would happen if this was resolved? How would it improve your world? What would be the impact on your team and your business?

The small stuff is easy for us to focus on. Small stuff is often in our area of expertise. Our skills have developed to the point where it doesn't take much mental effort to accomplish them and move forward. Unfortunately, small stuff often fits in the category of "unimportant."

It's not that the big decisions are that much harder, but they may take a little more effort than the smaller ones. They are often very important because big decisions have a bigger impact on the organization. The effect of a hundred small-stuff decisions may only add up to a tenth of a single big-stuff decision. Focus your time on the biggest issue first, and it may eliminate a number of smaller decisions you need to make.

See the Big Picture

Too often, people get caught up in the minutiae rather than seeing the bigger picture. If you need an example, watch the news during an election campaign. For instance, what does a woman's choice in wardrobe have to do with her abilities as a political candidate? The answer is absolutely nothing. Instead of focusing on her leadership track record or vision for the country, province/state, or city, our media outlets debate why the candidate wore a red versus blue scarf.

If you can focus on the big picture, it will greatly help your team. When the big picture becomes clear, the details are much easier to see.

What decision(s) or project(s) am I procrastinating on, delaying, or avoiding right now?

_____
_____
_____
_____
_____
_____

What question, if asked and answered, will help me resolve the biggest decision or issue I am dealing with at this moment?

_____
_____
_____
_____
_____
_____

When I resolve this current problem, what will the impact be on me, my team, and my business?

_____
_____
_____
_____
_____
_____

VALUES

When your values are clear to you, making decisions becomes easier.
— *Roy E. Disney*

30. What you value is what you expect

If you've ever heard the phrase "You get what you expect," it is very true. On the negative side, if you expect someone to be lazy, cheat, steal, or lie you increase your chances of getting that kind of behavior from them. In a positive light, if you expect them to be productive and positive, and achieve great things, you will more often get this behavior.

This concept can work purposefully, yet it often works negatively because we do not understand our own values, and we expect what we value. If you feel frustrated with a colleague, examine your "should" statements. Let me explain.

When someone is not performing the way we expect, we start creating a story in our minds about what is happening. Though fairy tales start "Once upon a time …", in real life they often start with a person's name followed by "should have _____." The word "should" is loaded with expectation, and is a great indicator of what we value.

Examining your Should Statements will help you better determine your values.

Examine Your Should Statements

Who	Should Do What	Your Value May Be
Jenny	Should get back to clients in 24 hours	Customer Service
Borden	Should come to me with ideas for how he wants to solve problems	Self-initiative and autonomous action

It is important to know what we value. Our values shape our lives, provide meaning, and help us make decisions in challenging circumstances. Take a moment right now to write down a few of your values. What principles guide your life, and what do you value in your relationships, work, or calling?

Values:

_____
_____
_____
_____

Knowing what you value is important as a leader. It is what you will expect of your team, though they may not share that value.

The trap happens when a leader has not shared their values with their team. I've often seen when a team member fails to meet an expectation or live up to a value, only to be reprimanded without understanding what the original problem was.

Nick and Bill are a great example of mismatched expectations. Nick is an extrovert and extremely outgoing. He likes to drop in, share ideas, and have strong discussions about them. Bill, on the other hand, likes to reflect on a topic in advance and prepare his thoughts, as he believes he can present better information this way. In this example, Nick values discussion and instant feedback in conversation. Bill, on the other hand, values reflection and preparation. Both can work together, but the styles will be in constant conflict until they realize what they value. Nick needs to discuss ideas in order to improve and expand them. Bill needs time in advance before responding. If Nick can give the topics in advance, he will get a robust discussion with Bill and both can be fulfilled.

Actions

1. Identify your values. Reflect on what is important to you. When you last got angry, what was the reason? Chances are, something you valued was overlooked or violated. When you last felt happy, what were you doing? What were those around you doing? This may reflect your value. If you are in a relationship, there are probably a number of situations that happen repeatedly that elate or infuriate you. Reflect on these situations and you will begin to see what you value.
2. Prioritize your values and share them with the people in your life. Ensure that your family and colleagues are aware of what

you value so that they know what your needs are.

3. Have the people in your life identify their values and share them with you.

When you are able to identify your own values, you will start to see what others around you value. It will help you as a leader to understand what they need and how to give and get the most from them.

One last informal story illustrates this principle. Our friends, Chris and Jen, were out of town camping with their family. As can happen when traveling, they forgot their toothbrushes. They weren't too concerned as they stopped in a town, and, while Jen was exploring the library with the girls, Chris went to get toothbrushes. When he returned, Jen was shocked that he had purchased toothbrushes priced at $7 apiece. Normally, she purchased whichever discount brand was the least expensive. She asked why he purchased this type of toothbrush, and he said it was because he likes the brand and it feels good when he brushes. This is a terrific example of how two individual's values vary and, therefore, their expectations vary. Chris values brand and comfort while Jen values low cost. Jen assumed Chris would pick up the toothbrush type she always did because that is what she values; however, he picked up the toothbrush based on what *he* values.

31. Use Stories to Communicate Your Values

Now that you have thought about your values, it is important to communicate them. The question then becomes what actions to take to embed these values in your team culture.

Values Statement

At the top of your corporate identity, do you share what the values are? Are your values reflected in your brand identity, communications, and formal documents? Are they listed before you present your vision, mission, or other guiding corporate statements?

Policies and Procedures

How do your policies and procedures reflect your values? When advertising a new position, how does the job posting attract candidates that share your values? What interview questions do you ask when hiring? How are they demonstrated in the way you manage the organization?

If official documents don't do a good enough job of communicating values, what is a better way? I recommend using a system that humans have been using before we had the ability to write. This system not only communicates ideas but also propagates itself. Further, your message will reside in the memory of your team longer and have a much more lasting impact than a statement on the wall seeking to seem aspirational. This process is storytelling.

Use Stories to Communicate Your Values

- Stories of successes and failures
- Stories of individual or team heroics
- Stories of decision making and impact

Some believe gossip was built as a tool by humans. It allows for quick dissemination of information while bonding people together (or excluding them) based on shared values. A great example of this is demonstrated in the movie *Basmati Blues*. An American scientist for a large agribusiness visits India, where she is testing a new strain of rice. Everywhere she goes, the people already know she is coming. The locals call this gossip network Rice Paddy Radio. Can you think about a time you experienced the equivalent of Rice Paddy Radio?

Part of the reason that this works is that people are gossiping about stories about other people. Have you ever heard employees or colleagues gossiping about mission or vision statements, policies, or strategic documents? Chances are you haven't, though everyone knows the juicy news about the latest promotion. What if your organization shared stories that reflect your values and were shared as quickly and ubiquitously as news on Rice Paddy Radio?

Stories are a powerful and primary method of communicating culture. Consider how you can use them to communicate your values and use that power to bind your team together.

Identify the Stories in Your Organization

What stories (no matter how big or small) do I have at my workplace and what values do they communicate?

Story
_____
_____
_____

Values Communicated
_____
_____
_____
_____

INFLUENCE

The key to successful leadership today is influence, not authority.

— Kenneth Blanchard

You may be wondering how you build a strong organizational culture when you're not the President of the company. The good news is that you can have a lot of influence without authority. When you take accountability, communicate, and set your leaders up for success, you will gain a lot of influence within your organization and make changes along the way.

32. Manage Up

It is easy to get caught up in our own world. We focus on our problems or concerns. At the same time, we believe others, especially our supervisors or other leaders, know everything we are doing and thinking. This just isn't reality. There is more going on in an organization than one person can monitor. The good news is that you can help your leader and your team by Managing Up.

Much of the focus of leadership books and strategies is top-down. How does a leader influence their subordinates, their team? Little is written about serving the leaders to whom you report. As a leader, your role is to serve and influence both up in the organization as well as down. This section focuses on how to give value to your leader in order to increase your influence with more senior leaders in your organization.

Make Your Boss Look Good

As a young professional, I was told that it was my job to make my boss look good. My initial reaction was indignation. Isn't my supervisor supposed to support me? As I grew up, I came to understand what this statement means. It's not always about vanity, image, or reputation. It's mostly about effectiveness. When you make your boss look good it means:

- You are communicating the highlights, challenges, and activities of your team well.
- You have prepared your supervisor to answer questions intelligently, which reflects positively on them and your entire area.
- Your team looks good because you have called attention to their successes with your supervisor.
- Your likelihood of receiving support increases because you have built trust with your leader.
- You and your area are more likely to get recognized because your boss is going to share what you've told them with their boss.

Activity

Put yourself in your supervisor's position. What do you think they want to know? What would they want to share with their supervisors? What would make them look good? If you were in their position, would you only want to hear problems, or would you want to know about highlights and achievements that you can praise and promote to your supervisor?

As a leader, make your leader's life easier. It's not sucking up. It's serving effectively. When you keep your leader informed, it serves your team. This is an opportunity to highlight their skills and problem-solving acumen. Reporting up serves your clients, as you and your team may be closer to them on a day-to-day basis than your boss. It serves your boss because you are preparing them with great and relevant information that they can use to report up and showcase your area. You look prescient if you are pointing out problems and the solutions you've enacted to solve them.

Poop Rolls Uphill

There is an old business saying that "poop rolls downhill." It means that when there is a problem the trouble rolls from the leader to the next level in the organization and all the way down to the most junior colleague.

In our modern world (and it's probably been much longer) I find that it is the exact opposite. "Poop rolls uphill." In fact, problems defy gravity. They almost fly up the hill of responsibility to the top office. When something goes wrong, who do your clients blame and want to talk to – the CEO, President, Director, or the person with the biggest title? If you are low in the organizational pyramid, you may have to help solve a problem; but the public isn't usually screaming at you the same way they are at the leaders higher up in the organization.

If poop rolls uphill, you want yours to be sweet smellin'. There will be problems you need to pass up the leadership chain, and that is OK. Solving problems is the majority of business activity. Listening to only problems all day, however, can be exhausting. Consider the burnout rate in psychiatrists and mental health professionals. In a 2017 survey, Medscape noted a 42 percent burnout rate for professionals working in these roles. Listening to problems all day is challenging. Fortunately, there is a way to improve this for everyone; to balance out some of the challenges we experience with positive moments that remind everyone what great work is being accomplished.

Tell your supervisor what they are doing well and what you appreciate about their leadership. Praise is something leaders will often pass along to their staff, but no one thinks to praise the leader or acknowledge them. You are training your leader as much as they are training you. The better you communicate what you need and what you appreciate about how you work together, the better your relationship can be and the more effective you will be working together.

Weekly Report on Activities

Be proactive and provide a brief summary of the activities of your area each week to your supervisor. Unsure what to share? These questions may help.

Who is someone in your area that is performing well or has done something special recently?

What goal has your team achieved for which you are really proud?

What problem has your team solved in a creative way?

What information might be useful for your supervisor, senior leaders, or other colleagues in the organization to know?

What are the results of a recent initiative?

What would be a great opportunity for inviting the leader of your organization to come to a meeting and praise your team? (When did you last ask your leader to do this? When will you ask them to do this next?)

Take Responsibility. Don't Blame.

Your leader has tremendous influence on the quality of your work experience. For this reason, it is easy to blame them when you are dissatisfied. If you're not having fun, it's the leader's fault. If you weren't recognized for your great work, blame it on the supervisor. If you're not getting what you think you need or want, the leader must be responsible.

I'm not saying that your concerns are not valid; there may be real problems. However, assigning blame to the leader is the easy way out. It allows you to step back from responsibility and complain. If something happens, great. When nothing changes, you still have something to complain about.

If you are not getting something you need from your supervisor or the work situation, first consider what you are doing to get your needs met. It's easy to put the expectation on another person, but how can you take accountability to improve the situation?

If you feel you or your team are not being recognized, how are you communicating your achievements? Are you communicating your achievements? If you would like more fun in your workplace, what suggestions are you and your team making or modeling that might be adapted or adopted more broadly?

You have more influence than you may realize. Start by considering your role in the situation. Are you blaming, or are you working to educate your leadership in order to gain desired outcomes?

As a young professional working at a small college in West Virginia, my teammates and I thought it would be positive to spend some additional time creating a strong team connection. It would be easy to blame the supervisor for not setting this up for us. Instead, my colleague, Jason, began to organize a Friday lunch club. It wasn't complicated. We got together for lunch on Fridays. Sometimes, someone would cook. Our supervisor was invited and participated. It turned into a very positive activity that boosted morale and connection and didn't require our supervisor to approve or organize.

Benefits of Managing Up

When you take the initiative to make a situation better and communicate that to your supervisor, it has multiple benefits for you and your team. First and foremost, it will make you stand out as a leader and someone who has an impact in the organization. It models to your leader as well as your team that change is possible and that they are capable of it too.

Among colleagues in the organization, you may find a lot of people will appreciate your efforts and recognize your ability to get results. This builds social capital for you that can be used when you need assistance in the future.

In addition to the recognition you receive, your leader and your team will both receive recognition for the positive results being accomplished in your area. Thus, your effort to Manage Up creates a multiplying beneficial effect.

Leaders Can't Invite Themselves

Here is one last lesson to remember. Leaders can't invite themselves. You have to invite them.

If your leader hasn't joined you for one of your meetings or attended an event or function that was important to you, it doesn't necessarily mean they don't care. It might mean they didn't feel invited.

There are power dynamics involved between leaders and their team members. If the team is planning an activity, the leader doesn't know if they are included. If you want your leader to be involved, you have to invite them.

I've seen many leaders who don't want to impose on their teams when their teams want them to be involved. Inviting your leader to spend time with your team is a great way to connect them to the people and increase their familiarity with the work of the unit.

33. Create Your Own Career Plan

If you want to advance in your career, there is no better way than to create your own career plan. Though there are no guarantees of advancement, there are steps you can take to put yourself in a position to do well.

The first step is to realize that your supervisor, whether it is a team leader, director, president, or CEO is most likely a busy person. Even if this person is terrific and supports you, they have a lot going on as they have a broader scope of responsibility.

The next step is the realization that you are responsible for your own learning and development. Many people expect their supervisor to be able to automatically recognize their needs for development and growth. A "wait and see" approach like this puts your life firmly in the hands of another. That is great if you trust them, but as the previous point illustrates, leaders are busy. Waiting on them can slow down your career development. Taking ownership of your career is the fastest way to advance it.

To do this, create your own career plan. Reflect on what you want and where you would like to be in your career and business. Once you are clear on what you want, it is much easier to pull together a plan.

Refine the plan with the specific actions, experiences, and resources that will help you achieve your career ambitions. Is there additional training you need? Would a specific mentor or advisor help you? Are there certain meetings or committees that would be useful for you to attend? Ask yourself what experiences you need to develop the understanding that takes you to the next level.

The second part of the plan outlines what support you need from your supervisor. Perhaps they can introduce you to key people. Maybe you need them to authorize the training you desire to take. You might need support with time away, or you may want to shadow them.

As you prepare to advance in the organization, this can raise a dreaded question for your supervisor. "What do I do when you're gone?" Currently, you are probably doing a good job and you are definitely filling a need. If you want to advance, your supervisor may be concerned with how to fill the role you are leaving. If you want to present a really advanced career plan, fill this gap. Propose your plan for how your responsibilities will be covered. Perhaps you have someone who would be a good replacement and you propose to train them to step into your role. You may also see ways to reorganize or share your responsibilities among other areas of the organization. Consider the impact on your supervisor and organization when you advance out of your current position and offer ways to mitigate it. Create a solid plan and make it easy for your leader to help you advance towards your career or business goals.

Where do I want to be in my career or business in the next five years?

_____
_____
_____
_____
_____

What training, contacts, meetings, experiences, events, committee involvements, etc. do I need in order to grow toward my career or business goal?

_____
_____
_____
_____
_____

What support do I need from my supervisor/leader to help me with this plan?

_____
_____

How can my current responsibilities be covered when I advance to a new position in the organization or as I grow my business?

_____
_____
_____
_____
_____

34. Treat Everyone Like They Are a Member of Your Team

How would it change your approach to the way you work if you treated everyone like they were a member of your team? How would you greet them? What questions would you ask? How would this change your view of developing others?

It's easy to focus on those that report directly to us, but what about the custodian contractor who cleans your office space or the receptionist at a client's place of work? Have you considered how you can improve the sales rep who sells your software or train the consultant you recently hired to do your social marketing? How would it change your life if you were able to train your supervisor to supervise you better?

Think of the number of people you interact with in order to successfully run your business. Whether they work internally or externally, if they get better will it make your life better? If you made them better, would your job get easier?

I want to challenge you to think beyond the group you supervise. I want you to consider your team in a much broader way and consider how you can help those folks improve.

Consider inviting them to train with you. How would they benefit if they attended a training session with your team? Imagine a stronger relational connection with your team members. This can provide an improved understanding of your operation. Further, it shows a good will and commitment to the other person that is bound to reciprocally benefit you.

Have you ever asked if you can give someone feedback? I strongly recommend this. Some may decline and that is OK. You can't push feedback on others if they are not ready to hear it, but many people are hungry for feedback and will appreciate it. They want to get better and serve better. If you offer them feedback, most will appreciate it, and as they improve, they can better work with you.

Activity

List all of the people (outside the team that is accountable to you) that you work with on a regular basis or who impact the work you do.

_____
_____
_____
_____
_____

Reflect on each person. If they were to change their behavior or take one action that would improve your performance while benefiting them at the same time, what would it be?

_____
_____

When will you approach the person to offer to give them feedback, so they can serve you better while at the same time making them a stronger professional?

___

35. Always Look for Talent

The best executive is the one who has sense enough to pick good men [and women] to do what he wants done, and self-restraint enough to keep from meddling with them while they do it.

— Theodore Roosevelt

Good leaders hire for needs, but great leaders hire great people. Good and mediocre leaders post a job when a position opens and wait for applicants. Great leaders seek out their next team members before the job exists. Good leaders look at their current team. Great leaders look for their next team members. Good leaders wait until there is a vacancy to hire someone new. Great leaders find a way to bring talented professionals onto their team in advance to support new and exciting goals.

Our businesses and workplaces require a lot from us. For that reason, the hiring and selection of new staff is often delegated or left to departments like Human Resources. You may not feel you have the time to think about the next generation of the team until you have a vacancy, but the best time to start thinking about your next team member is now. You may not have a position for them. You may be unsure about exactly how they can help you. It doesn't matter. If they are talented with a positive attitude, keep them on a list of top recruits. When you are ready, seek them out and tell them you want them to apply for the position. Telling someone they are wanted is a powerful motivator and increases your chances of hiring them.

Often candidates are seeking an employer, but how powerful is it when the employer seeks out the candidate? Keep in touch with gems you come across in your professional world. You never know when you might hire them.

Look for the Person; Not the Position

We are slowly coming out of an age of outdated leadership and organizational models. For quite a while, literature treated people as parts of a machine; and you can see this in the way that hiring is done. Often a job description is drafted and then you look for the person who can be that cog in the machine. Though a certain baseline of skills may be needed, this can overlook the fact that talented people who are committed to learning can be a great asset. They may not be exactly what you are looking for if you want all the boxes checked, but a great person can have a monumentally positive impact on your team and performance. Then again, someone who checks the boxes may fit the job description but may not have the excellence you are looking for.

Hire the Best

In a previous role, I created a new leadership position for my team. I had a great person who worked for me that was in line for the position, but we differed in our style and delivery on expectations. During the interview process, another excellent candidate interviewed for the position. This was someone I didn't know, but she was outstanding in her preparation and presentation during the interview and follow-up conversations. It was not an easy choice to make, but I chose to go with the new person. I thought she had the right talent for this position; after working with her for a number of years, I found I was right. She was phenomenal and someone who proved it repeatedly.

It may be difficult but hire who you think is best for the position. Great leaders hire the best people they can. When I was in graduate school, the Vice President of Student Services taught one of our courses, and he told us to hire people better than we are and get out of their way. I have always found this to be true. Great team members make you look great, so hire the best.

You Can Always Work With Those Who Want to Learn

Someone once told me that the most important attribute they hire for is attitude. After hiring and working with thousands of professionals, I understand this statement. I'm sure you do too. It's much more pleasant working with someone who has a good attitude.

The corollary to this is that you can always work with someone who wants to learn. Obviously, there may be some specialized skills or training that are a prerequisite to certain positions. That is understandable. However, most positions require a new employee to learn before they are fully effective in the organization. Even college and university graduates don't go straight into jobs with full knowledge of what they need to do. There is a lot of on-the-job training and experience they need to gain before they become proficient in their role.

At this moment, you don't know everything you will need to know in one, five, or ten years. There is much you will need to learn as a leader and much your team will need to learn. If you look to hire learners for your team, they can grow. If they can grow, they can adapt. If they can adapt, your organization will be successful for a long time.

Great People Reflect on You Greatly

Insecure leaders worry about competent staff. Instead of seeing them as valuable, they see a talented colleague or employee as a threat to their position. Interestingly enough, the opposite is true.

When you have great people working for you, they do great work. This is what your leaders see. They see your capacity to bring together a group of high performers. This reflects well on you. When leaders at the next level in an organization see this, they will consider giving you more responsibility, not less. They want you to bring this level of success to more of the organization.

It's Hard to Advance if You're the Best

If work is only about what you can do, it's hard to advance. In order to get the most out of people, it requires leadership. True leadership means giving trust to your people and mentoring them to grow as leaders. If you do not train leaders to come after you, how can you rise as a leader? If you are promoted, you will need leaders to replace you. Certainly, you can hire externally, but if you've trained your people, you have the next generation of known and proven leaders readily available to you. This provides continuity and strength in the organization.

To be the best as a leader means having the best team. To have the best team requires you to focus on developing leaders and trusting them to grow and get the work done. If you are the only one who can accomplish the work in your area, how will you ever be able to advance beyond your position?

If You Hire Great People, Anything Is Possible

I firmly believe that a great team can go anywhere and be successful. A great team is not about technical skills. It is about cohesion, communication, execution, and accountability. A great team can learn together, challenge each other, and serve at a high level. Technical details can be learned, but teamwork, real teamwork, comes from experience and commitment to each other. With those qualities, anything is possible.

ACCOUNTABILITY

Responsibility is a unique concept... You may share it with others, but your portion is not diminished. You may delegate it, but it is still with you... If responsibility is rightfully yours, no evasion, or ignorance or passing the blame can shift the burden to someone else. Unless you can point your finger at the man [or woman] who is responsible when something goes wrong, then you have never had anyone really responsible.

— *Hyman Rickover*

As a coach, one of the most common areas of help my clients are looking for is accountability. Often, they do not know what this means for them. Do they want to pay me extra if they fail to achieve a goal? Are they expecting a tirade on my part? Is it sympathy they seek? Most people are surprised that accountability is not about any of those actions. Granted, those can be used for tools in the process, but they won't necessarily result in action.

Accountability is always about asking the hard questions. At the core, it is asking if agreed-upon tasks were completed. If they were not, accountability requires the exploration of why they were not completed. This can lead to powerful insights into the thoughts, beliefs, and behaviors that hinder performance. Awareness improves our ability to be accountable to future commitments.

36. Never Take on Someone Else's Problem

Never disrespect someone by taking on their problem. If you do, it communicates that you do not have faith in them to solve their own problems. When you leave that person with the problem, you respect their creativity and capacity for solving it. Further, if they take your solution and it doesn't work out, now they will blame you. This hinders the maturation that comes from making their own decisions and experiencing the consequences.

If you take ownership of the problem, you may experience negative side effects as you have added to your own list of responsibilities, likely increasing your stress, and put yourself in a precarious position because you may or may not have the capacity to deal with this issue. You may fail at your own job responsibilities because you have taken responsibility and dedicated time toward work that your colleague should be doing.

To avoid this, ask the colleague how they would like to handle the problem. Add another level of accountability by asking when they will take action towards fixing the problem. In this way, it keeps the responsibility for a solution with them and prevents you from being burdened with a collection of issues that take you away from the problems you are tasked to solve in your own work.

The Three Questions of Accountability

By asking three questions, you can keep accountability with the person presenting the problem.

What are you going to do about it?

When will you take action?

What do you need from me?

With these three questions, you have firmly left accountability with the other person while offering assistance. You did not say you would solve the problem. You did not make any promises. You did not sympathize or join them in blame, shame, or whining. This sends a powerful message.

First, it doesn't let the other person off the hook from their responsibilities. Second, it communicates your belief in their ability to resolve the situation. Third, it shows your support for them in coming to a resolution. Fourth, it puts a timeframe on the response.

Deadlines Create Accountability

Speaking to the last accountability question, it is important to ask when the person will take action to resolve their problem. Many people will wish to come to you to complain. It may be a sob story, or it may be a legitimate issue. Those who want a true resolution will appreciate a timeline. It makes the situation real. Contrarily, those who are simply whining will not like a timeline for the same reason. It makes the situation real.

When a timeline is attached to an action, this takes the problem from a theoretical exercise and transforms it into a tangible result. A timeline demonstrates that you take their concern seriously. It places accountability on them to make a change, and it also puts leadership accountability on you to follow up and find out if they followed through.

In writing this book, I engaged an accountability partner. He was writing his own book at the time, and we agreed to hold each other accountable as we both wanted to finish our projects and thought this would be a useful tool for doing so.

In setting up our accountability partnership, we helped each other identify our next steps and agreed to follow up with the other person on what actions they had taken since our last meeting.

Initially, this was great. I set my goals in such a way as to build momentum. Each week I hit new milestones, and I enjoyed reporting back on my progress.

Further into the project, my motivation lagged. This was the time I didn't look forward to our accountability meetings. I didn't want to report that I had missed my target.

I am lucky, though. My partner lived up to our agreement and he always asked me about my progress. This forced me to assess what was happening and to find ways to resolve it. He couldn't do the writing for me, but he held me accountable by asking the difficult questions that forced me to follow up and follow through.

Reflection:

List all of the current projects and tasks you are working on. How many of them truly belong to you?

Consider your past week. What conversations resulted in you taking on a problem from someone else?

On a scale of 1 to 10, how much accountability do you take for other's problems versus keeping accountability with that person?

1 = I take on others' problems. 10 = I keep accountability with the other person.

1_____ 5 _____ 10

Keep Accountability Near the Source of the Problem

Don't let your team begin a habit of coming to you for answers or decisions on everything. When a problem arises, it often will not require your level of attention. Assess what is happening. Occasionally, it may require your resources, but often it will be a problem that is challenging your staff and that they are capable of handling. As often as possible, keep the responsibility for solving the problem closest to the source of the problem. There are two reasons for this.

First, that colleague has the most information about the problem. If it is a complaint, they have already heard it. If it is a technical issue, they most likely have the greatest level of knowledge regarding the technical needs. If it is a human relations issue, it may be an area of growth for them to address it.

A second reason for those closest to the source to solve the problem is that they are often more knowledgeable about solutions for the problem. Ultimately, it affects their work directly. If they are given accountability for the solution, they will find one that works for them. If a problem is solved too far from the source of the issue, the solution is often not satisfactory to those whom it affects. Have you ever seen the effect of a solution handed down from the corporate head office that didn't work for the colleagues on the front line serving the customer?

There are numerous benefits to this as well. Every time you allow your team to solve the problem, it shows confidence in them. This in turn builds trust. Trust is reciprocal and showing trust in the team will also build their trust in you.

This principle also creates faster decision making and reduces response times. When your team understands which decisions they need to make, versus the ones that really do need to come to you, response times drop. Those needing decisions are getting them faster because the team understands their role in making them.

Another benefit is that it allows you to keep your focus on your own work. Instead of solving everyone else's problems, you are able to keep your eye on the big picture. You can solve the problems and pursue the opportunities that require your attention.

Keep accountability close to the source of the problem and you will get better answers in a shorter time frame.

Accountability Is Your Job

As a leader, accountability is your job, but it doesn't mean that you are responsible for taking the corrective actions. You are accountable for an outcome but often it will be the role of one of your team members to accomplish the necessary tasks that lead toward that outcome. What is most important is that if a problem comes to your attention, you ensure that it is moved toward resolution.

When I was leading a university housing operation a number of years ago, the department had a vehicle that was used for various professional errands, transportation of supplies, and the various tasks a company vehicle is used for. One day, one of my managers made a comment about the vehicle being unsafe. She thought she was making a joke, but I took her comment very seriously. If the vehicle was unsafe and this was brought to my attention, it had to be addressed. I am not a mechanic and therefore not the right person to address any vehicle problems, but I was able to have my maintenance team check the vehicle and ensure it was safe for regular operation. This is an example of a problem brought to the leader. The leader takes accountability, and the appropriate person resolves the problem.

What is most difficult as a leader is trusting in your team when you are accountable for the result. It is important to remember that though the solutions your team will devise will be different than the choices you might have made, they will work well; maybe better than what you would have created. Delegation is a challenging task for most leaders. It is one of the hardest skills to develop as it requires letting go of the responsibility for doing the work while maintaining accountability for accomplishment.

37. Ownership of Communication

In a relationship, there are various levels of ownership in the communication that takes place. To be an effective leader and encourage your team to take initiative, consider these three levels ownership related to communication. At what level do you and your team communicate with each other and clients?

Level 1 – Blame the Other Person

At the lowest level, there is no ownership of communication. It is easier to blame the other person for not understanding what you feel you clearly communicated. Instead of looking into the matter, you consider the other person a (fill in the blank pejorative) and do all in your power to let your supervisor and team know that this person is not doing what they are "supposed" to do. You can identify Level 1 Communication by the number of excuses you hear.

This is often demonstrated in relationships. For example, Chris is upset. Pat can see that Chris is upset and inquires as to what is wrong.

Pat tells Chris, "You know" without telling Chris what is actually wrong. It is easier for Chris to blame Pat than to explain what is upsetting and allow an opportunity for both people to take ownership in resolving the problem.

Level 2 – Recognize That You and the Other Person Are Equally at Fault

It is a sure sign of maturity when you recognize that, in any relationship, you are part of the problem. If you are not getting what you want from the other person, it is time to reflect on what you are asking and how you are asking it.

Activity

Roleplay with a mentor or trusted colleague a conversation you had and ask them what they understood about what you communicated. I highly recommend recording this and reviewing the video, as this helps you notice what you did well, where you can improve, and what is missing from the conversation. Repeat this action multiple times and you will begin to get a sense of your communication patterns and habits. Awareness will give you the opportunity to overwrite these patterns with new, more effective, communication habits.

Level 3 – Take Ownership for the Communication Between You and Your Client

Level 3 is true service to your client. Excuses do not exist here. This is not a reactive space. In fact, it is the exact opposite. Level 3 communication is thinking about the client and asking them the questions they haven't thought of yet.

You are an expert at what you do. Just because your client has hired you doesn't mean they are an expert at what you do. That is why it is powerful when communicating with them to ask them questions based on your experience.

Consider the common questions you've received at each stage of the process of delivering your product or service to them. This will give you insight into potential areas that may be blind spots for other clients. You have the advantage of making these known to your client in advance and setting everyone up for a more successful engagement.

What is the benefit of taking ownership of communication? First, it makes you look like an expert. Most clients will be ignorant of some aspect of your service or product delivery. Many won't know exactly what they want, or they may be poor at communicating their expectations. When you take ownership of the process and ask questions they may not have considered, it shows your expertise. Second, it makes them comfortable because you are obviously the expert who knows more than they do. You look smart, capable, and credible.

Activity

Common Misunderstanding or Topic of Miscommunication	What question can you ask in advance with a client to mitigate this problem?

What service has been most appreciated by clients? This might be a way to add value to your client if they have not asked it of you and you deliver on it.

_____
_____
_____
_____
_____
_____

Don't Wait

Another aspect of taking ownership is the refusal to wait on another person, partner, subcontractor, client, etc. for information, action, or follow-up.

I worked with a client who was frustrated with his team about their follow up. When he asked his staff about the status of a project, he was often told, "We're waiting on the customer to get back to us." This did not serve the team, the customer, or the business. Through our coaching, he learned to train his team to take the initiative and follow up with customers rather than wait for or expect a response.

It's important to remember that customers and clients are busy just like you. They may get distracted and forget your request for information, yet they will still want you to fulfill your commitment as agreed upon. Make their life and yours easier by owning the communication and reaching out instead of assuming they will initiate contact with you, which leaves you waiting for a response. If they haven't met your deadline to reply, don't wait any longer. It's likely they have another priority that superseded your request. When you connect, it demonstrates the care you are putting into the project and your commitment to completing it as agreed upon.

Questions for Consideration

What often comes up when working with your clients or customers? What solutions work best? How will you incorporate this into your sales or customer relationship management process? How can you provide value before your customer asks for it?

What information can you give the client early on to make it easy for them to respond to you? How can you front-load your communication to make it easy for the other person to respond with a decision?

38. Sins Versus Mistakes

Growing up, I attended Catholic church with my family every Sunday. The homily (sermon) was usually focused on humans as sinners. A sin is when you break a rule of the church. Thankfully, it is something for which you can be forgiven, but there are consequences. As I've gotten older, I've realized I can take some of my experience growing up and apply it to my leadership experience. Sin is one of these concepts.

I was a new professional working in West Virginia when I began to realize the difference between a sin and a mistake. I believe that we need to allow people to make mistakes, and I gave thought to what a mistake really is. A mistake is when we make an error or choice that yields negative results. It usually happens as a result of limited knowledge or experience on behalf of the decision-maker.

On my teams, I expect my colleagues to make the best decision they can, given the knowledge they have at that moment. (Really, can anyone do better than this?) If the outcome is negative, this was a mistake. If we can learn from it, it is a mistake. If the decision or action was aligned with our values and didn't work out, this is a mistake.

A sin, on the other hand, is something different. A sin occurs when you know the values of the organization and choose to make a decision against those values. Theft is a great example. If someone steals from your business, that is a sin. You can forgive the person, but there are consequences. Trust has been broken. Values were violated. This may not be a circumstance in which this person can remain a colleague.

To prevent unintentional sinning in the workplace, it is important to understand your values and to communicate them with your team. How do you make decisions? What are unbreakable principles for you when it comes to how you operate and fulfill your mission? What is a breach of trust versus a learning moment? To set your team up for success, they need to know and understand the expectations.

As a leader, it is not only to your benefit to follow up when someone has sinned. Your team expects you to do this too. If a team member has sinned against you or the organization, it means they have sinned against the team. This means the team will have lost trust in that person, and consequences are to be expected as the colleague breached agreed-upon values. If you do not follow through as a leader, you will lose the respect of your team since they look to you to maintain the agreed-upon standards. If you do not follow up, it communicates that these values aren't important, and that diminishes the sense of belonging to a greater whole.

When a colleague makes a mistake, the team can often forgive this. Team members appreciate that they may make mistakes in the future. Showing compassion and tolerance for mistakes models to the entire team that it is OK to take risks.

Working with your team, think in advance and share with them your values. Give them examples of what constitutes a mistake and what you consider a sin so that they know their boundaries and understand where you draw the line.

Activity

If you haven't identified your core values already, go to the section of this book that will help you do this.

Write your core values.

_____
_____
_____
_____
_____

List some mistakes you've made or witnessed.

_____
_____
_____
_____
_____

What are some examples of when you've sinned or seen someone else sin (violate organization values)?

_____
_____
_____
_____
_____

What would you consider the worst betrayal from a staff member?

_____
_____
_____
_____

How would you handle this situation with the staff member?

_____
_____
_____
_____

How would you respond with your team following a situation where another team member violated your values?

_____
_____
_____
_____

39. Know the Difference Between Whining and Complaining

There are two kinds of responses to problems—whining and complaining.

Complaining is a good thing for your organization. When someone brings a complaint, it means they have identified a problem affecting your business and they want to solve it in order to improve the situation for everyone. They may have found a gap in your service, project, or operation. If you've created a culture where it is safe to complain, it will allow you to respond proactively. This puts you ahead of the problem and puts you in a position to explore multiple options for its resolution. After the problem has manifested, your options narrow. You and your team may still be able to overcome it but handling it reactively will be more challenging.

When a team member complains, expect them to bring solutions. They may require some assistance in refining their ideas, but providing an initial solution means they are committed to the work you are doing and want to improve the organization. A colleague who has a complaint maintains accountability for resolving the problem. This is what a professional does.

On the other hand, you may be working with a whiner. This is not much fun. Whiners want to tell you about their problems without taking any accountability for solving them. They desire to offload responsibility using excuses, misdirection, and blame. Often, whining is a technique used to try and garner sympathy or pity or distract from poor performance. Use the Three Questions of Accountability listed earlier to hold the whiner accountable. Do this repeatedly and they will stop whining to you.

As a leader, encourage your team to communicate problems and monitor the line between complaining and whining.

MEETINGS

A strong leader meticulously plans and methodically orchestrates meetings in order to achieve a desired result, or he doesn't hold them.

— Roger Stone

Meetings are the number one least-liked aspect of work, yet people don't want to get rid of them entirely. They just want them to be better. As meetings continue to be a large part of the work environment, here are some tips and tricks to make them better for everyone, especially you.

40. Bringing Purpose, Productivity, and Meaning Back to Meetings

I've attended meetings that I've loved and meetings that I've hated. How about you? Analyzing many discussions with colleagues about meetings, I've identified a common set of reasons that cause frustration around meetings.

- No purpose
- No agenda
- No clear outcome from the meeting
- No accountability from prior meetings
- Attendees' time is not respected
- Talk around an issue without addressing what is truly important

Meetings don't have to be hell. Use some of the following methods to bring meaning back to your meetings.

Purpose

Always have a purpose for your meeting. If it is not clear why the meeting is scheduled, it doesn't need to happen. Meetings aren't about disseminating information so much as asking important and powerful questions and discussing as a team how to solve them. Identifying the purpose of the meeting forces you to focus and really consider what you are trying to achieve. It also centers the attention of the members of your team. When they know why they are meeting, they can better direct their energy toward that topic, and the meeting will be more productive.

Prepare

Meetings are mostly taken for granted whereas they can be a source of tremendous value. Many leaders call a meeting without preparing for the meeting. Scheduling the meeting is only one step in creating a successful meeting. To get the most out of everyone's time, it is worthwhile to schedule time in advance of the meeting to plan for the meeting. Consider what you want to discuss and what information will be useful to the team prior to your discussion. Taking the time to prepare and communicate this in advance will improve the quality and outcome of your meetings.

Value Your People

Many meetings are used for updates, which is a waste of human capital. We have various tools such as e-mail or Microsoft Teams for this kind of data dump. The real benefit of gathering your team together is to take advantage of the collective creativity to solve problems, plan for taking advantage of opportunities, and create, sustain, and enhance your work culture. Don't waste time if it's just an update that could be emailed.

Once Around

A well-used method for ensuring everyone's potential involvement is to leave time at the end of the meeting to do a "once around." A once around is simply asking each person if they have any final thoughts on the topic of discussion. It allows all those around the table to participate, especially if they have been quiet up until this point. If they have nothing to add to the conversation, they may pass.

Use a Charter Document to Enhance the Purpose

While I was working at the University of Calgary, I was asked to chair the Subcommittee on Primary Prevention of Sexual Harassment and

Violence. From the title, you can probably tell the scope of this committee was quite broad. There are any number of initiatives that the group could work on related to preventing sexual harassment and violence. To avert us from straying from our purpose, we developed a charter.

Very simply, a charter is a brief document (I prefer one page at most.) that outlines the purpose, membership, and desired outcomes of the group. Additionally, it may include any relevant conditions, restrictions, or resources as well as a timeline for the work to be done. It is the compass that guides the work of the group.

Drafting a charter focuses your group. It details the purpose and parameters within which they will be working. This saves precious time for all the members of the committee. It prevents confusion and provides an anchor that can be referred to when the group is getting off track.

Having a charter for the subcommittee I chaired allowed us to focus on our short and long-term strategies and create a program from which all could benefit.

Clarify and Assign Accountability

Have you ever left a meeting feeling like nothing was accomplished? This often happens when those who lead the meetings have not practiced the skills of managing a meeting. Thankfully, the skills for managing a meeting are the exact same skills used for listening effectively. If you want to manage meetings better, I recommend taking training or getting coached on active listening. Until you do, here are the two skills to practice that will rapidly increase the effectiveness of your meetings.

Clarify

When there has been enough discussion, summarize back to the group what you've heard. This is your opportunity to achieve two important goals. First, it allows your team to feel heard and demonstrates that you have been listening to them. Second, it is a final opportunity to ensure you understood what was discussed before proceeding. Both of these are positive for your team culture and the quality of your decision making.

Assign Accountability

Once you have clarified the discussion there will often be a takeaway—a task that requires action. You may assign this task to someone if you wish, or you can ask who will take on the task. This gives your team a chance to step up and take ownership and accountability. They may need the help of other team members, and that is understandable, but you need someone to be assigned accountability for the task. Nothing gets done without a name attached to it.

End Early

Don't be afraid to end early. If you have fulfilled the purpose of the meeting and exhausted your agenda, it is OK to end the meeting. In fact, many, if not all, of your colleagues will thank you. Like you, they have many other responsibilities and will appreciate the unexpected time. Further, this gives you credibility as a leader for having the ability to stay focused and respect everyone's time.

How Do I Know When It's Over?

The best way to know your agenda is exhausted is that each item has been discussed and you have created a specific actionable item, assigned one of the team with responsibility for its accomplishment, and set a date for when this item should be completed.

Another indicator is if you are hearing the same ideas shared. Anytime someone begins repeating what has already been said, it is often an indicator that the conversation has been exhausted and it's time to make a decision.

If there are no further questions that need to be answered in this meeting or as a takeaway from the meeting, you are done. Now it is time to let everyone get to work.

Ownership of the Meeting

Have you ever attended a meeting where the person who called the meeting does not attend? Worse yet, have you ever found yourself in a room of colleagues and no one knows who is supposed to run the meeting? Perhaps you've been in a room with a group of colleagues who are all reluctant to run the meeting.

Though a source of understandable frustration, the good news is that this is a curable meeting affliction. If it is not clear who is running the meeting, choose to take control of the meeting yourself. Until someone "owns" the meeting, the group can't take ownership of the meeting either. Once leadership is established, it allows all members to take ownership and participate.

It may seem daunting to lead such a meeting, but often all you have to do is start by asking a question.

Possible topics to address when attending a meeting with no identified leader of the meeting:

- What is your understanding of the purpose of this meeting?
    - This may give you more information, or you may find out that no one really knows why this meeting was

- called, which means you can cancel it and gain time back in your schedule.
- Since we are together, is there anything we should discuss that would have value for all of us?
    - This allows you to take advantage of the mistake in case there are topics of value you want to discuss with this specific group.
- I recommend we reschedule for next week. I will follow up with (insert name of the most appropriate boss or next person higher up in the organization) and cancel the meeting if it is not needed or ensure an agenda is sent.

When you take ownership of a meeting, you will act differently. You can now facilitate the meeting, ask questions, clarify responses, and identify actions for follow up. Your colleagues will often go along with you as they are looking for someone to lead the meeting. If you called it, you lead it. Certainly, you can share the chairing of a meeting. Many successful teams have done this, but they all identify who is leading the meeting. Once this is identified, it makes the rest of the meeting run much smoother, and everyone can now own it as "our" meeting.

Keep It Fresh

Repetition has its uses, such as working to master a new skill. Repetition also has a downside. When we repeat an activity, it is easy for our minds to wander. Meetings are much like this. When the meeting agenda or content never changes, it is more difficult to pay attention to the meeting. Therefore, I recommend you Keep It Fresh.

Keep it fresh simply means vary the agenda, topics, activities, or mood of a meeting. It is easy to follow a set agenda each week. It takes little time to prepare, but it doesn't bring any energy to the meeting either. When you introduce a theme, game, different agenda order, special guest, trivia, or any of an infinite number of possible changes, it gives energy to the meeting. It also triggers the brain to pay attention as we are biologically wired to note novelty.

The good news is that it doesn't have to take a lot of time. You don't have to come up with all the ideas yourself. Have your staff take some responsibility. This is a great way for everyone to improve their creativity, and it will carry over into other areas of work.

Meeting Structure

If you already have a meeting structure that works for you, that is great. If not, consider the following as a general structure to use for promoting conversation without limiting discussion. This is not the best or only way to run your meeting. It is a template. Be brave, make adjustments, try different ways of running a section, add or remove a part of the meeting that isn't working for you and your team. Meetings aren't meant to be static, and they often change as the team, organization, or situation changes.

Prior to the Meeting

- Consider the purpose of the meeting and the desired outcomes.
- Create and share an agenda of desired discussion items.
- If it is the first meeting, consider creating and distributing a charter that outlines the purpose, membership, and desired outcomes of the group.

At the Meeting

- State the purpose of the meeting. This will focus the minds of those in attendance. Focused attention will yield much better results.

- Review the agenda and ask if there are any items anyone would like to add.
- For each agenda item, state the problem or opportunity and give relevant context. Providing supporting information will help with problem resolution.
- If you have an idea, be the first to share it and allow the team to mold and shape it until you've created the solution that works best. Sometimes it helps the team to have an idea to build on instead of having to come up with a brand-new idea from scratch.
- Ask the team for their feedback and thoughts on solving the problem. This can be a discussion, brainstorming solution, take away and report back activity, or any other process that works for you to promote the sharing of ideas among the team.
- Summarize the key points. People can get distracted in conversation and it can lead them in many directions. For this reason, it is important as the leader to listen intently and to summarize what has been said. This creates clarity for you and the group, and it provides one last opportunity for members to correct a misunderstanding.
- Make a decision and assign accountability. Always, always, always assign a person to be responsible and a deadline. Without these two crucial components, no action happens.
- Move onto the next topic.

After the Meeting

Summarize the key decisions, actions, and accountabilities in an email to your team. Drafting this gives you one more chance to reflect on what was discussed, and it provides an accountability reminder to those who attended.

At the Next Meeting

Review the action items from the previous meeting and ask for updates on progress if they haven't been shared already.

Get PAID

Productive meetings can result in big payoffs. To remember the basics of better meetings, use this acronym and get PAID.

P – Purpose. Ensure there is a clear purpose for the meeting (the *Why*).

A – Agenda. Have a list of questions that will be asked and topics to be discussed (the *What*).

I – Invite discussion. Ask questions and promote open discussion with diverse points of view (the *How*).

D – Delegate and Deadline. Ask who will take accountability for following up on each action item and when (the *Who*).

41. Start With an Idea

In Violence Threat Risk Assessment Training, Kevin Cameron teaches that most offenders are imitators, not innovators. Similarly, in nonviolent and everyday situations, people are much like this—prone to copy or build on something that exists rather than start from zero.

Fortunately, you can improve the performance of your team by starting them with the seed of an idea. The final solution may look entirely different than what you proposed. Be open to that, but if you propose an idea initially, others can build off of it. It's not important for the first idea to be "right" or even effective. What matters is that you start the dialogue, which gets the group thinking.

A Snowman Starts With a Flake

When you see a snowman, you are seeing the final product of a number of decisions. Yet how did that snowman start? You might think it started with a snowball, but we can go back further. No snowman can come into creation without snow. What is snow but a collection of snowflakes? When we share a starting idea, it is much like that first flake of snow. Together we gather up a pile of snowflakes and crush them together into a snowball. As we consider larger possibilities, we begin to roll that ball into a snow boulder, which will become the base of our snowman.

When I started, I wasn't sure how we would build our snowman, but I knew I had a cold flake of water and wanted to bring other flakes together to create something spectacular. My team then added their knowledge and creativity to create a process to fuse a snowball and create a snow boulder. I didn't have to know everything, but I had a basic idea; then as a team, we were able to build on it together. Eventually, we built a surfer dude snowman. It was not what I expected. It was much more interesting.

If I had told my team to go outside and do something spectacular, the instructions would be pretty vague. They are all talented and I'm sure they would figure something out, but it would not have resulted in building a snowman.

A classic example from history is that John F. Kennedy didn't know how to get a man to the moon—he only believed it was possible. He didn't start by telling his team to think of something big for his country to do. Instead, he gave them a clear starting point. On May 25th of 1961, here are the words he used to provide the initial vision of what would indeed become a defining event in human history.

> *I believe that this nation should commit itself to achieving the goal, before this decade is out, of landing a man on the moon and returning him safely to the Earth.*
>
> — John F. Kennedy, Moon Shot Speech

It doesn't have to be a moon shot for your team; it can be much more down-to-earth. But consider providing your team a starting thought so that they can expand on it to solve the problem in an incredible way.

LEADERSHIP HACKS

> *Excellence is not a destination; it is a continuous journey that never ends.*
>
> — Brian Tracy

Hacking is a term that originated in the computer science field. In mainstream culture, it is often thought of as meaning to illegally break into a software system. This was not the original meaning of the word. What it actually referred to was the process of reducing the amount of code needed to achieve the goal of a computer program.

If you think about writing a book, the first draft may be huge. There is often a lot of extra material or ways to present ideas using fewer words. As a result, the editor and author hack away what isn't needed, to get to the essence of the story.

I consider myself a pragmatic person, and I always want my clients to leave our conversations with tools, tips, and tricks – hacks, you might call them – for making their lives easier. In this section, I provide some hacks that will help your productivity, communication, and effectiveness as a leader. They are not theoretical, and you can apply them right away.

42. A Few Tips for Being More Efficient

There are many ways to accomplish your work. Consider taking some time to learn some tips and tricks to help you be more efficient. Find what works for you and apply it. Here are a few ideas to get you started.

Start Small

You may have heard the phrase "Dream Big." That is a grand idea, but the bigger the goal or dream, the harder it is to get started. Having an outrageous goal can be good if it inspires, rather than intimidates, you; but a big goal can seem daunting and cause procrastination where action is needed.

In order to build momentum, consider starting small instead. Reduce key activities into easily achieved chunks. With each successive mini-task you complete, you build momentum toward your goal and belief in yourself to accomplish it. Once you have momentum, it is easier to see how the goal can be attained.

Writing this book is a great example. I thought about writing a book for many years before finally getting started. It wasn't until the first meeting with my writing accountability partner that I had a metric I could measure in small amounts in order to build momentum—words per day. As I started, I committed to writing twenty words a day (with a day off in the week). I had no idea how many words I could write in a day, let alone a week, and as I tracked my progress I noticed something astonishing. I never wrote 20 words in a day. It was almost impossible for me to write 20 words in a day. I always wrote more! Some days a little more and others a lot more, but I always wrote more than 20 words a day.

Soon, my goal increased, and I began with weekly targets. About a month into the process, I noticed that I was writing around 2000 words a week. It wasn't long until my accountability partner challenged me to write 3000 words per week, and I hit that target. The progress was amazing. It led to the creation of this book, and the entire process started by committing to writing 20 words each day!

Learn How to Type

What I have found astounding over the years is the number of people who do not know how to type. An inordinate amount of work and non-work life revolves around computers. Yet, many people use valuable time to hunt and peck out the letters rather than becoming skilled at typing.

If you haven't already, I recommend you teach yourself to type. There are numerous websites that provide free lessons. You can learn on your own time. It doesn't take a lot of time each day, and once you learn it you will continue to get better since you are practicing these skills as part of your regular work activities every day.

Personally, I type faster than I write. This skill has served me any number of times and, more importantly, has saved me a great amount of time.

Using OneNote or EverNote

Would it be useful if you were in a meeting to have the minutes of the previous meeting on hand? Would it be helpful to have the latest floor plans of the building you are designing in easy access to show a client? When someone at a team meeting is unsure what you decided previously, would it be useful to be able to quickly reference what was said?

Instead of having to search through folders and different drives, consider a program like OneNote, which allows you to keep all the information in one place. Your company may already have similar tools. Take some time and learn how to use them. These can bring together all of your notes, files, and relevant materials in a searchable connected space.

Time Management

Calendars are often misused or underutilized. A calendar program is simply a tool to help us manage our time. Like any tool, if we use it correctly, we can gain from it tremendously.

Step one is to realize that your calendar is not meant only for meetings. In actuality, it is a way of tracking our priorities by tracking our time.

Consider your priorities and what you need to accomplish. Go to your calendar and schedule these priorities into it by using blocks of time. Treat your project time like a meeting in order to have the time to do the work that is important to you. This will also make it harder for others to book you solid (especially if you have an assistant managing your calendar) because you already have blocked out these times in your calendar. Essentially, this is creating a meeting with yourself to work on your priorities.

In your schedule, include time for your various activities:
- Strategic planning and thinking
- Project work
- Responding to e-mails, calls, and communication
- Family activities
- Personal activities—exercise, hobbies, etc.

How we spend our time is how we communicate our true priorities. If we don't schedule what is important to us, our time will always go to other people's priorities. Manage your time or others will do it for you.

Text to Confirm Your Meeting 2 Hours in Advance

Where you work, you may have a culture in which people are consistent in showing up for meetings. If you are an entrepreneur or in sales, you may have found that people are less consistent. To reduce the amount of time wasted by a client, colleague, or partner missing a meeting, text them at least two hours in advance to confirm the meeting.

Why two hours? Two hours is usually ample time for them to confirm with you and can save both of you some travel time.

Many phones will have shortcuts for messaging. I recommend creating a shortcut that will load a template response that you can update with the time of the meeting.

This may seem an unnecessary and annoying habit, but if it saves you an hour in your week when someone didn't show for a meeting, isn't it worth it?

Manage Your Inbox

You don't need to respond to every email you receive. In fact, you don't have to act on every email you receive. When going through your inbox, get rid of all of the easy emails—quick deletes, yes/no response, file for information, etc. For the messages that will take some reflection or require consideration or prolonged action, schedule time in your calendar to respond and file the email to be responded to later.

Events

For emails that have information that expires after a certain date, create an Events (or whatever name suits you) folder. This allows you to clear those emails out of your inbox and know where to find them if you need the information later. As the information for these emails expires after a certain date, you can periodically clean out this folder.

E-mails Requiring Action

Emails that require further action can be placed in an Actions folder. This is your follow-up folder for the items you scheduled to follow up on.

An Empty Inbox

Processing your inbox quickly twice a day gives you more time to work uninterrupted. It allows you to clear your inbox while planning for when to respond to the various items requiring your attention.

How freeing would it be to have an empty inbox?

Consider Not Using Your Inbox as a Task List

Some professionals I've known like to use their Inbox as a Task list. I do not recommend this for two reasons. First, it is easy to lose track of what you are supposed to respond to when it sits in a list of hundreds of emails. Second, it can be mentally overwhelming when your Inbox has so many emails in it. This can impact your level of stress, performance, and focus. Use your Inbox for what it was intended—a temporary place for communications to you.

Rules, Rules, Rules

There are wonderful tools in most email management systems that allow you to create rules for processing messages. For instance, if the President of the company sends you a message, you can flag it with a color, a specific indicator, or even a ... flag. On the other hand, you may receive a regular update that is not urgent for you to read. A rule can move it directly into a separate folder you've flagged for later review.

Using rules to manage your email can reduce your Inbox load by redirecting low priority and non-urgent items while at the same time signaling you to important messages. What rules would help you manage your email?

25 and 50-minute Meetings

The default length of time for most calendar programs is one hour. Reflect on the past week of meetings you had. How many required an hour? How many could have been much shorter?

One way to gain time back is to change the default amount of time you use for your meetings. I recommend 25 and 50 minutes. Essentially, this reduces your half-hour and one-hour meetings.

Reducing the time allotted for the meeting will increase the need to get to the intent of the meeting. Because it is outside the standard duration for meeting times, it will communicate to the other participants that you are busy, and that will help you keep the meeting on track. As most meetings are scheduled on the hour or half-hour, shortening the meeting also gives you more time to transition between meetings, take notes, or relax for a moment before starting your next meeting.

Because these are not the standard length for meetings, others will take notice. It will stand out and you will create an opportunity for everyone to respect each other's time while discussing what is important.

Consider how much time is really needed to accomplish your objectives. How often will 25 minutes suffice? How many meetings need to go for a full hour? What if you can accomplish the purpose of the meeting in under 50 minutes?

Set your expectations early by scheduling shorter meetings.

Activity

For the next week, schedule all of your meetings into 25 or 50-minute blocks. Note what happens. Were the meetings just as effective? More effective? How did your colleagues respond? If you like the results, how will you make a habit of scheduling your meetings in this way?

Avoid Waiting for Others

There are times when we have to wait, but I recommend you never do so when you can avoid it.

When the service technician tells you they will be at your house between 1:00 pm and 7:00 pm, you don't have much choice. You need their services, and you will need to wait.

When this situation comes up with people you know, you don't need to fall into this trap if you are clear from the beginning. Therefore, never put yourself in a situation where you are waiting for others to contact you within a range of time. Instead, choose a specific time.

If you agree to an open window of time, it will take away your focus and ability to be present with what you are doing. In the back of your mind, you are thinking about this indeterminate interruption. You know it is coming but not when, and this prevents you from giving a task your full attention.

When someone says they will call between 2 and 4 pm, here is a way to respond. "That's great. I'll put you in my schedule for 2 pm." When you get specific, they will get specific. When you set a specific time, it also communicates that your schedule is important. Your life is not on hold in order to make yourself available to the other person. You have your own schedule of important activities. Schedule specifically to allow you to focus intensely.

No Purpose? No Way

If someone wants to meet with you, always ask about the purpose of the meeting. If they are unsure, don't meet. If the purpose of a meeting is not clear, the likelihood that the meeting will be a waste of time is very high.

Unfortunately, this happens often. Someone will invite you to a meeting. The request only has a title and often the title is not very descriptive. No information is provided in the meeting request notes. The header might as well say "stuff", as you have no idea what it is about.

If there is no purpose, agenda, title, or information about the meeting, it indicates that your colleague has spent no time considering these factors. That means they are willing to waste your time in the meeting trying to figure out what they should have communicated to you in advance.

For that reason, I recommend that if there is no purpose or agenda for the meeting, don't attend.

Train Others by How You Handle Your Time

When you manage your time, you will teach others around you how to work with you. When you schedule your priorities, others will work their meetings around yours. When you shorten your meetings or require a meeting agenda before committing to attending, it trains your colleagues to better prepare before engaging you.

You don't have to be the supervisor, director, or president to have an impact. Choosing to manage your time sets an example for all those around you. When you work differently, your colleagues respond differently.

43. Networking. It's Not Just for New Jobs.

Networking is an important skill that applies to more than job hunting or sales calls. It is also crucial to you as a leader within your organization.

Ask yourself who you work with, and you may automatically think of your team. This is natural, as they are the ones you see most frequently. In reality, you probably work with a much broader base of people. If you are in a large organization, there are definitely others outside your scope of direction that have an impact on your work. If you are a small business or organization, you may already understand all the benefits of networking as you rely on others outside your business to survive and thrive.

Regardless of your circumstance, consider developing your networking skills. Here are a few tips.

Networking events aren't for getting to know people. They are an expedient way to gather contact information for a number of people. The most important activity is gathering business cards. Don't plan to make deep connections or forge significant work or business relationships at the event. People are on high alert—too conscious about what they think they should or should not be doing and, therefore, not paying real attention to what you are saying to them. This is not the ideal event for making true connections.

The Follow Up Is Where the Magic Happens

Whether you are looking for a job, trying to connect with a future client, or building a relationship within your company, it is important to remember that the real magic occurs in the follow up after the networking event. It is important to give the people you've met a call within 48 hours (preferably 24 hours) of the event while you are still fresh in their minds. You might be wondering what to say. There is no need to make it complicated. Here is an example.

> Hi _____. It's (your name). We met at the (name of event). I'm following up as we didn't have much of a chance to connect, and I was wondering if you'd be interested in getting together for coffee/tea (or whatever relaxed mode or venue suits you). I'd like to learn more about what you do and see if there are any opportunities for us to work together.

If the last phrase feels uncomfortable, drop it altogether. The important action is that you reach out to connect with this other person. Very few people follow up after an event, which is why you will stand out by doing so.

When you are able to meet with this person, now you are truly doing the work part of networking. This is when you will find out about them—their business operations, challenges, and responsibilities. What is different in this situation? To start with, you will both typically be more relaxed than at a big event. This allows you both to focus on actually developing a relationship, and you will listen much better and get to know one another. Second, you are building a personal connection. You never know how this will benefit you or how you can benefit the other person. It may not be immediately apparent what the benefits will be, but you will leave with a deeper connection to the other person, as they will to you.

Afterward, send them a thank you note. If there was a topic you connected on, mention it. If there is an opportunity to work together, mention that. This creates a third interaction with you. I've heard it said the average adult needs to hear or see something seven times before it is learned. I'm not sure if that is accurate or not, but if it is, you have just created three touchpoints (four if you include the follow-up call). How much more likely are you to be remembered? How much more likely is the person to want to work with you in the future?

Whenever I think about networking, I remember a student I coached. She was nearing the end of her university degree and she was looking for work. She was going to attend a networking event, but she was very nervous about it and unsure of herself. I coached her on how to get the most out of the event and to follow up afterward. She overcame her fear, followed through, and connected with a recruiter for a major Canadian bank. He attended lots of networking events, yet this student was the first person to ever follow up with him afterward. To make a long story short, they met for coffee, and guess what happened? She got the job.

This also works internally between colleagues of an organization. Once at an internal business event at the university, I networked and met a colleague named Billy who specialized in using fun and humor to improve performance. I followed up with him afterward; we got to know one another. When I was in need of a keynote speaker during team training, he volunteered. That wouldn't have been possible if I hadn't networked and followed up.

No algorithm can network for us, which makes it such a powerful activity. We are social beings, and we place more trust in personal connections than internet connections.

44. Download Your Thoughts

Have you ever felt that you weren't as present as you could have been when listening to someone? Ever felt distracted when working on an assignment? Part of this response may be that the topic is boring or the assignment isn't very interesting. On the other hand, perhaps you have too much going on inside your head, and it is time to download your thoughts.

Why does it help to download your thoughts?

Consider the computer. Every time we open a program on our computer it takes more processing power. This results in fewer resources focused on single activities and reduces the computer's performance.

Our brain operates much like a computer. We may start working on one task when a request comes along, creating another task that engages our mind. Our capacity for each task just dropped by half as our attention is split 50% for each task. Add two more tasks and our capacity is split again, with these four tasks each receiving only 25% of our mental attention. As more tasks, concerns, and ideas take our attention, our capacity for addressing each diminishes to the point where we accomplish very little while feeling increasing stress, worry, and distraction.

Imagine instead that you have one task and that is all that is on your mind. You can apply 100% of your mental power to it. This will help you to complete it more quickly, fully, and effectively.

Downloading our thoughts, which many call journaling, is a great way to reduce your mental burden in order to free energy for focusing on what is important. When you write down your thoughts, there are many benefits, including:

- It removes it from your mind, so you can focus your attention on your current priority.
- Having an idea written down saves it for future contemplation or exploration without having it constantly nagging in the back of your mind.
- Journaling removes the anxiety of forgetting the great idea you had.

- Writing is also a form of thinking, and you may surprise yourself with the many ideas that come to you as you draft your thoughts.
- This can be a reflection process helping to refine ideas, discussion topics, and great questions for problem-solving, finding opportunities, and adapting to changing circumstances.
- If the idea was a tiny spark, writing it down may help you clarify it into a blazing fire.

It is natural for thoughts to surface. Search for how many thoughts a person experiences in a day, and you will see numbers from 12,000 to 80,000. Whether sitting at our computer or talking to a colleague or friend, thoughts may arise. If you have a pen and paper handy, I recommend writing these thoughts down. Capture them so that you can return your focus back to what you were doing.

I use this process when meeting with others. An extrovert by nature, I often have ideas when I am in a great conversation with another person. Not wanting to divert my attention by leaving the thought in the background, I will tell the person that I am writing down an idea so that I can return my attention fully back to them and our conversation. It takes less than 30 seconds, and our conversation continues.

It's important to understand that, though we have thoughts that come to us unbidden, we don't have to deal with them in that moment. We can capture them to explore later when we have time or wish to make them a priority.

Capture Brain Sparks

Because I tend toward the extroverted end of the spectrum. I've come to learn this means that while I am talking with someone else, my brain is thinking. In fact, talking is helping my brain to think. One of the side effects of this is the stimulation of my creativity. I often find I have what I like to call "brain sparks." A brain spark is an idea that seemingly comes out of nowhere. It is bright and shines like a spark, yet the lifespan of it is short like a spark too. If I don't capture it, it fizzles out of my brain with no guarantee that it will spark again.

Develop a system for recording your brain sparks. Whether it is a pen and paper or a voice recorder app on the phone, note your idea so that you can come back to it. Many great ideas started because a brain spark at night was written down on a pad of paper next to the bed.

45. The Benefits of Practice

It is easy to see someone who performs seemingly effortlessly and believe they were gifted with talent. Though they may have some physical ability that contributes to their success, the majority of those who master their art do so through rigorous practice.

This is great news as a leader. It means you do not require a natural charisma or leadership skill set to be successful. You can learn the skills you need and practice them to improve your overall performance. With practice comes confidence. With experience comes competence.

The following are tools used to practice, develop, and enhance skill proficiency.

Roleplay

Roleplay is a great tool for two reasons. First, it allows you to practice as though the situation were real. Second, it makes most people extremely uncomfortable. This is great, as it brings real emotion to the activity. The more emotion you feel in practice, the more aware you can become of your own response to the situation. This will help reduce your anxiety and bring out less emotion when doing it for real.

For example, one of my clients made the decision to fire one of his staff. He was exceedingly nervous. In the past, we'd discussed situations like this, but it was not enough to prepare him this time. So, we role-played various scenarios. He was able to try different languages and approaches. More importantly, he became aware of how much anxiety he was feeling. As we continued to roleplay, his anxiety dropped. When it came to the time for the actual meeting with the employee, my client was almost relaxed because he had been able to practice in advance. Since he was not pent up with anxiety, it helped with the entire meeting.

Practice Like It's Real

In basketball, my coach would tell us to practice like it's a game. What he meant was to practice as though the conditions were real instead of merely a practice. If you practice with less intensity than you bring to a game, you'll bring that lesser intensity when it is game time. So, practice like it's real.

This concept applies to many different leadership activities. One example that comes up commonly is speaking in public. Whether at a town hall, board meeting, or product launch, this can seem daunting. Many people prepare their written notes and that is where they stop. They take those notes and read them, usually poorly, at their event. They forget to take the next step and practice like it is real. This requires rehearsing the speech by speaking out loud. It is different speaking words than reading them in our mind. For many, hearing the speech out loud will lead to adjustments in the content. When we speak, we use our entire body to communicate. This is why it is so important to practice with our entire body when we rehearse.

Practice like it is the real event and you will be prepared.

Break it Down

The greatest improvements do not derive from practicing everything but from focusing your efforts on specific small activities. In *Peak*, by Anders Ericsson and Robert Pool, they highlight that the greatest improvements come from finding very specific areas of focus and working on developing those micro-skills.

For example, a person can play tennis every day. They will get better initially and then their performance will plateau. To improve beyond this point, they need to identify specific aspects of their game and dedicate hard work to improving them. As they improve their skill in a focused activity, their overall game improves.

When practicing, consider what you want to work on and focus on that one activity. You may want to become a better public speaker, but that is still pretty general. Would you improve more if you knew that you needed to work on breath control, eye contact, posture, composition, or any of a myriad of skills related to speaking? How could focusing on one of these aspects improve your overall speaking ability?

Video Record Yourself

One of the blessings of living in a time when video recording is available on every device is that we can use that tool to improve our performance. There is no better tool for improvement than watching ourselves perform. Hearing someone tell us we are dominating a meeting is entirely different than watching ourselves dominate a meeting. When wanting to improve as a leader, have yourself recorded doing the activities of which you would like to improve. Be kind to yourself as you watch and analyze the playback. Remember that you are learning, and it is OK to make mistakes. In fact, if you are not making mistakes, you probably aren't trying hard enough. Learn from the mistakes by observing your behavior and you will rapidly improve.

46. The One-Step Method to Getting Started

I have coached many professionals on how to become public speakers. Most often, they want to improve presentations to their board of directors and investors or come across as more polished when hosting a town hall meeting for their team or promoting a product launch. In this process, I have learned the one, most important action that helped them get started. It wasn't reading a book. It wasn't writing their speech. It wasn't getting coaching. The one step that generates all activity is to <u>schedule that next activity</u>.

Whether colleagues realize it or not, time is the ultimate determinant of priority. Have you ever noticed how tasks that aren't scheduled are less likely to get done? It is because time and deadlines help focus our minds. Knowing when a project, speech, or work activity is due focuses our energy, thinking, and effort on achieving it by that deadline. If you have ever stayed up overnight, finishing a presentation or report, you understand this explicitly.

Going back to coaching others to speak, the first task I give them is to schedule their next talk. Once they know when they are going to speak, they can work backward, develop their content, practice, and deliver an outstanding performance. Until they schedule it, the project will be easy to delay for another time.

Consider your priorities and create your own deadlines for any task that is important to you.

Activity

Project/Task/Speech/Activity	Completion Date	Resources or Planning Required
------------------------------	--------------------	------------------------------------
------------------------------	--------------------	------------------------------------
------------------------------	--------------------	------------------------------------

47. Avoid "Hey, Buddy" Syndrome

"Remember that a person's name is to that person the sweetest and most important sound in any language."
— Dale Carnegie, *How to Win Friends and Influence People*, 1936

Picture this. You are walking down a hallway when you run into a colleague you recognize but you don't remember their name. They greet you warmly, using your name. Feeling a bit embarrassed, you try to cover by using a general greeting like "Hey, buddy" or "Hey there," but it doesn't create the same connection as if you could only have remembered their name. I call this Hey Buddy Syndrome.

To overcome Hey Buddy Syndrome, you can develop the skill of name memory. It will make your job infinitely easier, earn the respect of your teammates, and help you be more successful when working with others. You may be thinking "I'm not good at remembering names." Don't worry. By the end of this section, you will be.

MMT (Empty) Name Memory Method

Here is your crash course in becoming a name-remembering phenom. It's simple, and all it requires are three areas of focus—Mindset, Motivation, and Technique.

Mindset

When it comes to memory, Mindset is the belief that you can be better at remembering names.

Let me demonstrate. Are you good at remembering names? If you responded yes, you are in the 2% of people who've actually admitted to me with confidence that they are proficient at remembering names.

The most common response to this question is, "I'm not very good with remembering names." Guess what happens when you tell yourself this. You give your mind permission to take a vacation. This statement reinforces the habit of not remembering names, but it says nothing about your actual ability to remember names. It is an unhelpful mindset and an excuse for not remembering someone else's name.

The first key to changing your ability to remember names is to change your mindset. Realize that remembering names is not a gift of birth. Instead, it is the result of developing a skill. Indeed, remembering names is much the same as any other mental skill you have acquired. It takes practice, but it is achievable.

Affirmations

Affirmations are a great tool for rewiring your brain messaging. Reflect on how many times you've said you are not good at remembering names. How would your interactions be different if instead you had told yourself you are good at remembering names?

Telling yourself regularly that you are good at remembering names may feel a bit unrealistic, especially if your faith in your ability is low. That is OK. You don't have to tell yourself you are good at remembering names. Instead, you can try something like this:

"Every day I am getting better at remembering names."

This statement is much easier for people to accept. You still may not feel great at remembering names initially, but you are starting to reprogram your mind. Instead of seeing this as an impossible task, you are training yourself to see it as a possible outcome. As you train yourself to believe you can remember names, you will start to see results.

I once saw Ron White, a noted memory expert, recite the names of an entire audience at a 400-person conference. What I will always remember is that he was not born with any special skill or ability. He worked hard training his mind to remember, and that has led to him becoming a top memory expert in the world. Imagine if you could remember the names of everyone in a room of five, ten, twenty, or even a hundred or more people. How would this make a difference in your work and your business?

Motivation

Earlier I quoted Dale Carnegie, who noted that a person's name is immensely important to them. The more important question, though, is why is it important to you to remember people's names? If you have a reason or purpose for accomplishing something, you are more likely to achieve it. Name recall is similar. If remembering names is not important to you, you won't do it.

When you think about the people in your life who are important to you, do you remember their names? What is the difference in motivation between remembering their names versus the names of others you meet?

If you are looking for motivation, consider this. What would happen if I told you that you had to learn everyone's name at a meeting by 4 pm? How does the motivation to remember change if I said do it or you're fired? What if I said to do it or you will lose your life? What if I said do it or you will lose a family member's life?

Those last examples are a little extreme, I admit. If you think about a person's name being the most important sound to them though, how does that change your motivation to remember their name?

Activity

Why do you want to better remember names?

_____
_____
_____
_____

What motivates you to want/need to remember names?

_____
_____
_____

How will you benefit at work, in your business, with your community or family by remembering other people's names?

_____
_____
_____

Technique

There are many techniques for remembering names. I have collected a number of them over the years and will share some that have been used with great success.

Facial Recognition

I learned this technique from Ron White. As a species, we are highly visual when it comes to our memory. We are also highly emotional. Both of these factors can contribute to a better memory when it comes to names.

When looking at someone, choose a feature on their face. It may be their nose, glasses, a mole, ears, forehead, etc. Choose what you think is the most distinctive feature and assign their name to it. More than that, add motion, sound, or other sensory perception to it. Take it to the next level and anchor it with an emotion.

Here are a couple of examples...

I have a friend named Siva who shaves his scalp bald. When I first met him, this feature stood out to me, so I imagined beads of sweat dripping off his head and when they landed, they sizzled his name---Sssssiva, Sssssiva. This visual, with movement and sound, helped me to remember his name.

Another time, I was at a conference with a new group of colleagues. As we went around the room, I used this technique with a gentleman named George. George wore thick, black-framed glasses (a throwback to the '70s style). I used these glasses to anchor my memory and imagined that they were giant slinky glasses. Each time the eyeglass would pop out it sounded out his name Geooorge, Geooorge (kind of like a boing! sound). Though I rarely see him, I remember his name to this day because of that simple technique.

Association

Though science continues to explore and seeks to better understand how our brains operate, it has been noted that we build upon what we already know. This is important and useful as we don't have to create new ways of remembering someone if we can associate them with something we already know.

For instance, I was attending a Toastmasters meeting when I met Luznel. She is a vibrant and fantastic person, though that is not what helped me remember her name. During an introduction, she shared her love for arepas, which is a fried corn biscuit-like food. I love arepas too and this connection allowed me to remember her name.

Spelling

When meeting someone, ask them to spell their name. For some, hearing the letters helps them visualize the letters in a way that cements them in the mind.

Sing It!

In one seminar, a young man told me he uses the person's name in a song, and I've used this when explaining how to pronounce my daughter's name. We blessed her with an uncommon name. Uniqueness has its advantages, but it can also come with some challenges. As her name is not fully pronounced phonetically, it is often mispronounced. Her name is Nimue. Not knowing how to pronounce it, many people say Nim-yu or Nim-ooh. In fact, her name is pronounced Nim-ooh-way. Fortunately for her, there is a song that is well known called "The Lion Sleeps Tonight" originally done by Solomon Linda. The chorus is "a weem away a weem away ..." I replace this with "Nim-away, Nim-away" and it has helped many to remember and pronounce her name correctly.

Write It Down

A simple technique is to write down the name. Keep a list or journal. Write down the person's name, where you met, and something you learned about them. Reviewing the list will help you to remember the person and their name.

I also recommend that you ask the person how to pronounce their name. Next to where you wrote their name, write it phonetically based on your primary language. For instance, I would write down the name Nguyen as Win, which is how the pronunciation sounds to me. Another example is Wojnarowska, which I spell phonetically as voy-nah-ro-ska. As you can see by these examples, pronunciations sometimes differ greatly in a native tongue.

Finding Further Techniques

There are many techniques for remembering names. If you would like to find more methods, consider the following:

- Observe who in the groups to which you belong are good with names. Ask them what name memory techniques they use.
- Conduct a web search. There are numerous resources for remembering names. Do a quick search and try three different methods that appeal to you.

Practice, Practice, Practice

Name memory is a skill like any other. Practice it regularly and you will get better.

When All Else Fails ... Be Humble

Imagine you're improving at remembering names. It's getting easier, but one day a person you recently met or perhaps someone you haven't seen in a while comes up to you and you are unable to remember their name. Don't panic. It's OK. It happens. You still have one tool in your arsenal---Be Humble.

If you don't remember their name, own it. Let them know you've forgotten and ask them to share it with you. Though there is sometimes disappointment, I've never seen a lack of forgiveness. Most people consider themselves poor at remembering names; for this reason, they are very willing to forgive someone who has forgotten their name.

I sang in a choir when I was in university. I knew everyone in the choir, but I had forgotten one woman's name. We were four months into the school year when we began working together to produce our Madrigal dinner show. I could not remember her name, and she was the only one in the choir whose name I didn't know. We were working on the set one day and I decided to correct this. I apologized for forgetting her name and asked her to share it with me. She did. Moreover, she thanked me for having the humility to ask instead of pretending to know or using some nonspecific greeting.

When you ask someone their name and admit to forgetting it, they know you have taken a risk. Your asking shows them that you are interested in who they are, and people love it when you take an interest in them. If you forget a name, be brave. The results may surprise you.

Find Your Way to Better Name Memory

There is no right or wrong way to remember another person's name. Find what works for you. Some methods may fit your strengths better than others. Remember that this is the easy part of remembering names. The most important action in remembering remains your belief in your ability to do so. Nurture that and you will gain the full benefit of any name remembering technique.

CREATING CULTURE

Corporate culture is the only sustainable competitive advantage that is completely within the control of the entrepreneur. Develop a strong corporate culture first and foremost.

— David Cummings

Focus on the Team

Organizations usually focus on how to make their product or service better, but who is focused on making the team better? The leader—

you. Too often, results are thought of separately from the team dynamic. They are seen as something that emerges on a financial report. What is forgotten is that results are the outcome of human effort. Without human beings contributing to the effort, there are no results. In fact, the human effort contributed toward a goal is what yields the results. Therefore, improving how a team and organization work will yield better results.

In the rapidly changing economy we currently navigate, organizations cannot afford to focus myopically on their product or service without improving their team at the same time. One is not separate from the other. Both are necessary. Who will move the team forward? It has to be you.

48. Office Morale

According to the Oxford Dictionary, morale is the confidence, enthusiasm, and discipline of a person or group at a particular time.

It is the sense of spirit, purpose, and drive in a group, reflected through its relationships. Therefore, you don't need extensive surveys to tell you about your staff morale—you can see it in the way people treat one another.

Greetings

Do people greet each other? This is may seem like the simplest activity, yet it is one of the most important and a key indicator of how your team may be feeling toward one another and the organization. Observe your team and notice if they acknowledge one another. Do they smile when they greet each other? If the environment is friendly, this is one indicator of positive morale.

In sports, it is common to see teams give each other a high five, where they slap hands with each other as an acknowledgment between teammates. It seems like such a small action, yet teams that provide this kind of acknowledgment tend to perform better. This is supported by research done with players from the National Basketball Association during the 2008-2009 regular season. In their article titled "Tactile Communication, Cooperation, and Performance: An Ethological Study of the NBA", Michael W. Kraus, Cassey Wang & Dacher Keltner found that touch led to improved performance, collaboration, and communication; all of which contribute to greater success.

Laughter

Every once in a while, stop what you are doing and listen to the office space around you. Is it silent? Do you hear anything? Do you hear laughter?

Laughter can be a good indicator of office morale. It shows a lightness of spirit and indicates that people feel safe in showing vulnerability through laughing. Laughter doesn't exist in closed cultures or environments with low morale, so if people are laughing, they are connected, and this is a positive attribute for your team.

Smiles

Numerous books speak to smiling and the fact that we are neurologically wired to smile in response to another human being. It's an acknowledgment that creates a connection with another person. If you see your team smiling at one another, chances are they have stronger relationships.

We Versus They

Listen to what language is being used among team members. If you hear the word "we" used a lot, it shows a level of engagement and identity in your team. On the other hand, the use of the word "they" can indicate disengagement or a lack of ownership and accountability.

What Can You Do?

It's easy to get distracted and to focus on our problems. You may forget to greet your team members, smile, or share a laugh, yet it is important for you to do so. As a leader, your team looks to you to set the tone of the environment. You can do this by modeling these behaviors. It signals to your staff that it is OK for them to do the same, and that will go a long way in creating strong morale within your office.

Activity

Visit a place where you can sit and observe the people in their workspace.

What do you notice?

_____
_____
_____
_____
_____
_____
_____

How often did colleagues greet one another?

_____
_____

How often did colleagues smile at one another?

_____
_____

How often did you hear laughter?

_____
_____

What did you observe and what do you think it means about their office morale?

_____
_____

49. Fun

Find ways to inject fun into your operation. In *The Influential Mind*, Tali Sharot explains that people actually think better when they feel safe and happy. Inciting fear leads to inaction, but creating a healthy, safe, and inviting environment actually helps colleagues bring better value to the operation. Adding fun to the workplace takes work. If it is not something you've practiced or you feel comfortable instilling, here are some suggestions:

- Find the fun people on your team. On every team, there is usually one person that everyone considers fun to be around. These people are probably bringing fun to your environment already. Now is your chance to ask them to do it intentionally.
- Consider a theme for your meeting. Work is busy, and this doesn't work for all meetings. However, choose a frequency – perhaps once a month or once a quarter – and use a theme for the meeting. The trick is that you can't just tell people the theme. You'll need to role-model, having fun with the theme. It doesn't have to be a ton of extra work, and you can choose how grand to make it. At the very least, consider wearing something aligned with the theme. If there is food, ensure it

is related to the mood you are setting. If the theme allows for stories or team-building games, utilize that to make them fun. It doesn't have to be much, but your team will come to enjoy and look forward to these meetings if they are having a good time.

- Change the format at work, in meetings, and one-on-ones. Have you ever noticed that most people who leave a training room on day one will return to the same seats for day two? This phenomenon occurs in many ways across our organizations. It is easy to get repetitive in our daily, weekly, and monthly interactions. Take a moment to do a Rut Analysis. Review all of your work activities. How are they the same every time? Once you have identified the repetition, consider how to alter those activities in order to make them more interesting. You might change the format or have someone else lead a meeting. Perhaps you would like to use a video or audio clip to demonstrate an idea. Whenever you do something differently, it has two great benefits. The first is that it wakes up your team. Humans are hard-wired to pay attention to novelty. When you act differently, your team will notice. The second benefit is that creatively changing your routines brings up the energy for everyone. You are presenting a new way of operating, and this is uplifting. New ways equal new energy.
- How can you greet people to make them think they are the best person in the world?
- Do you have dedicated space(s) for recognition? They can be great places for any member of the team to recognize someone else on the team. Specifically, they can highlight those colleagues who bring fun to the workplace. You can also use it to reinforce your organizational values by having

team members recognize when someone has acted in accordance with them.

Raising my daughter and spending time around kids taught me a valuable lesson—Kids LOVE Crazy! The goofier I acted, the more attention I received. This helped me a lot when trying to get out of the house. If you've ever tried to get a child to get ready to leave the house and they resist, you know how frustrating it can be. Once I learned to apply the Kids Love Crazy principle, my life got easier. I turned it into a game or competition. In a complete turnabout, leaving the house went from taking twenty minutes of getting our winter gear on to racing to catch up to my kid who was out the door before I was ready.

I share this with you to remind you that it is not only kids that love crazy. Adults like to have fun too. A little novelty in their lives is a great way to improve energy, creativity, and morale.

50. Overcome Power Over

As a leader, you have to recognize important lessons of power. The first is that we give power to others. It is not taken. It is something only you can give.

When your team comes to work, it has given some measure of power to you, as you have the choice to continue to employ the members or fire them from their jobs. They often forget that they gave this power to you, and they have the power to take it back if they no longer wish to abide by the employment agreement.

One of the former VPs I worked with used to laugh about how people viewed his position. He found employees looked to him for answers and felt he had power over them. In reality, he saw the situation much differently. To him, they each had the power to decide their own actions and contributions to the unit. He couldn't monitor and direct all of the activities of each person in his department. It's impossible. He relied on them to make choices that benefited the organization. He could tell them what to do, but they still have the power to choose if they will do it.

Losing Power

The quickest way to give up power is to let someone anger you. Often, we think our anger gives us power over the situation or the other person, when, in fact, the result is the exact opposite. When you become angered, you are allowing the other person to determine your response. In sports terminology, we would say they own you. You are not acting, you are reacting. Is there anything more grating than knowing you've given the person you are upset with power over you?

Blame is another way of losing power. If you blame someone else, you are giving away your power. In fact, anytime you blame others or fail to take responsibility for your actions in a situation, you give up your power to that person.

Choosing Our Response

I heard a great story that illustrates how easy it is to give others power over us. A journalist was interviewing a priest and the two went for a walk. On the way, they stopped at a newsstand as the priest wished to pick up the day's paper. The journalist watched as the store owner treated the priest coldly and callously, using some harsh language. He continued to watch as the priest smiled, wished the kiosk owner a pleasant day, and resumed walking with the journalist. The priest's smile never left his face.

The journalist was confused. He offered to go lecture the owner of the kiosk and put him in his place for the maltreatment he gave the priest. The priest graciously declined the offer. The journalist, not understanding the priest's calm demeanor, asked the priest why he didn't get angry at the kiosk owner. The priest equably replied, "Why would I let the owner choose my attitude toward the situation?" The priest understood personal power. At that moment, he chose his response rather than letting the owner's actions dictate how he responded.

51. Be Nice

Seeking wisdom from a senior leader, I asked what he believes makes for great leadership. He paused for a moment and issued only two words—"Be Nice."

He went on to explain that his father told him long ago that if you take care of the people, the people will take care of the business. This maxim has proven true time and time again. When your team feels respected and happy, there are multiple benefits for the organization. Productivity increases. Research done by the Social Market Foundation showed that an increase in happiness resulted in an up to 10% increase in productivity.

It doesn't stop with productivity. In her book, *Make More Money by Making Your Employees Happy*, clinical psychologist and bestselling author, Dr. Noelle Nelson, cites the following:

> A Jackson Organization study shows that companies that effectively appreciate employee value enjoy a return on equity & assets more than triple that experienced by firms that don't. Fortune's "100 Best Companies to Work For" stock prices rose an average of 14% per year from 1998-2005, compared to 6% for the market overall.

Being nice does not mean being a pushover. It doesn't mean allowing yourself or others to shirk responsibility. What it does mean is that you approach every conversation with warmth in your heart and kindness in your voice and actions.

Productivity and profit are two top metrics in business. If they, as the bottom line, are your objective, then being nice and making people happy is the way you achieve it.

52. People Need Structure, Not Stricture

In order to work effectively, your colleagues need some level of structure in their work environment. I know people along the spectrum from high structure to low structure. The one thing they have in common is that there is a base level of structure they wish to have in their organization. Even "low structure" isn't "no structure." By creating a common understanding, it allows everyone to feel comfortable exploring within an established set of boundaries.

Pretend there is a new project in your organization and a completely random set of colleagues is brought together to work on it. These folks have little or no knowledge of each other and are given zero instruction about how to organize themselves. I guarantee they will begin to create a structure within which to do their work.

We see this all the time. Consider kids on the playground. None of them may know each other but before you know it they are playing grounders (a popular Canadian playground game that is a variant of the game Tag) or another invented game. In order to play a game, you are required to have rules. Rules are structure. The rules don't hamper the game, but they make it enjoyable as they establish boundaries behaviorally and physically for the game.

Too much structure, though, constricts creativity. An excess of structure stifles the environment. People spend so much time navigating the structure that there is no room for the idea sharing and risk-taking that leads to opportunity.

On the other hand, too little structure can create frustration from a lack of process, delineation of organizational responsibilities, role clarification, clarity of purpose, or decision-making processes. It creates discomfort for colleagues who are unsure of their place in the organization.

Leadership is a balance. Provide a structure that allows people to share the best of themselves without stifling their spirit. Here are some operational aspects to consider regarding the structure of your organization.

- Set and regularly espouse the values of the organization. Your values drive decision making. When team members understand your values, it is much easier for them to operate autonomously and creatively.

- Talk about how you operate. Many orientation programs speak to what a colleague is supposed to do. However, it is just as important to cover how things get done. To clarify, this isn't about the micromanagement of a staff member. It's not telling them how to get their job done, specifically. You want to give them room to bring their creative self to the work. The how is about communication methods, decision-making processes, treatment of colleagues, and interactions with clients; what the expectations are about how each member of the team comports themselves in your organization.

- Problem-solving is a great example of a balance between structure and openness. A person's mind works best when building off of ideas. In solving a problem, you can provide a bit of structure while also leaving a lot of room for exploration. In fact, the structure can set up discovery. I've always loved this about brainstorming—a problem is shared, a potential solution is given, and then the rules are set to allow everyone to spew forth ideas. Through discussion, the idea is explored, modified, and reshaped—resulting in a better idea.

The Power of Post-Its

A great example of using structure to promote creative solutions is the Post-It activity. My previous team used to tease me about my love for Post-It notes (the notepad with the sticky residue on the back). At many of our meetings, I would run a brainstorming session. First, I proposed the problem or opportunity and gave some background information. Next, I gave one minute for each team member to write down their ideas, thoughts, or crazy intuitions—one per Post-It sheet of paper. After the minute (or two if they were really going), I had them put all their Post-Its on a wall, and we began to organize them.

I've done this exercise many times, and each time it is amazing to watch a group as they move the Post-Its around, find relationships between seemingly unconnected concepts, agree on ideas that don't apply to the topic, and group the Post-Its into tangible, workable solutions. The process is highly interactive and generates a great creative discussion that often yields better results.

Meetings – An Example

A great example of structure versus stricture is meetings. Meetings fail when there is too much or too little structure. Let's look at both examples.

Too Much Structure

When the process of running the meeting dominates the meeting, there is too much structure. Perhaps Robert's Rules of Order have run amok and more time is spent on misunderstanding or interpreting the rules that govern the meeting than on the core purpose of the meeting itself.

An overabundance of structure restricts members in one of two ways. It can make attendees at the meeting too nervous to speak up, thus restricting potentially valuable contributions to conversations. If a colleague is unsure about the process for speaking, they may choose not to speak at all. This means you will have meetings after the meetings where members will gather to discuss what they really think about what was proposed in the formal meeting. In essence, you create more work and discussion outside the regularly scheduled meeting because team members are cowed or confused by the high amount of structure in the meeting.

The other reaction it can evoke is boredom or disengagement. When a meeting is too highly structured, it is easy for members to get bored and to check out or withdraw mentally.

Too Little Structure

On the other end of the spectrum are meetings where there is little or no structure. Attendees may have no idea what the meeting is about or why they are supposed to be attending. A complete lack of structure creates frustration and can affect how the member feels valued by the leader or organization. A lack of structure can waste time when very few people feel they have time to waste.

BECOMING AN ADVANCED LEADER

It is not as much about who you used to be, as it is about who you choose to be.

— *Sanhita Baruah*

53. Coach Your Successor

As you grow as a leader, you have an equally important task. You need to coach your successor. This colleague may or may not end up taking over for you in this organization, but preparing them to take on your role has benefits.

It creates stable leadership for the organization.

It communicates trust and garners commitment from the team member.

It connects the team member to you as a leader. You may have a future opportunity to promote them or hire them away to a new venture or company to which you belong.

It demonstrates to the rest of the team a clear reporting structure and assurance that advancement is possible.

It role models leadership development for the leaders that report to you and encourages them to do the same for their team.

It allows you to practice the skill of training advanced leaders. This ability will always make you attractive as you advance in your career. If you can create leaders, you are able to take on more responsibility.

What if my protégé leaves before I promote them?

This is a great question. It may feel like you wasted your time and energy on this colleague, but you may instead find unexpected benefits from the process.

First, if you have dedicated time for developing a successor, it models that you care about the development of the people with whom you work. Others in your team will see this and be motivated, knowing that you believe in developing the people with whom you work.

Second, the colleague may have to leave for any number of reasons. Having been mentored by you, they will usually maintain a strong connection to you. This is advantageous as they will most likely remain in your professional circles. You never know when you will be able to partner with or hire them back after they've gained experience from another company.

Third, you create a reputation that will help you recruit terrific talent. Great people want to work for great people in a great environment. A culture that develops a successor is indicative of a culture that develops people. Motivated colleagues want to work in a culture where they can grow and learn. Once word gets out, you will get better and better people who want to work for you.

On teams I've led, we nurtured our colleagues, and many of them advanced, if not in the organization, then in taking on positions of greater responsibility in other organizations. We learned that colleagues talk to one another across the organization and soon my staff was being asked by colleagues in other departments if we had any job vacancies. They wanted to know if my staff would put in a good reference for them. The reputation of our team created a desire in others to want to work with us. This gave us great leverage in choosing who we wanted to hire. We were in a position of choosing those we thought best and most motivated for the jobs that were available. The new staff came in knowing of the culture of learning and development we had established, and they contributed to it, which reinforced the practices that built our reputation in the first place.

There are a lot of benefits of developing a successor and the rest of your colleagues. It demonstrates a commitment to your people that is rewarded in many ways within and outside of your organization.

54. Get Outside Help

There may be times when you wish to participate in a team conversation rather than lead it. If that is the case, consider hiring a third-party facilitator. It should be someone with experience working with groups and who is good at listening as well as asking clarifying questions. There are multiple benefits to using someone in this capacity.

It allows the leader to participate fully in the conversation because they are not facilitating the conversation; thereby they can focus their energy on the discussion and not split their attention between conversation and facilitation. This gives them an opportunity to contribute more as a peer. Further, the team may respond differently because it is not the leader who is facilitating the session.

The facilitator can ask questions that are difficult for the group to ask. Further, they can ask questions in an unemotional, curious, and care-based way because the facilitator has no emotional bias or political agenda. By naming the tough topics, the facilitator creates a safe space for discussing them. This can be especially useful as a leader if there is a topic that you would like to speak to without being the one to introduce it.

The facilitator will have a different style than the leader, which may allow for different results in the discussion. Team members may respond differently to a different style. Additionally, a facilitator can use any number of creative methods to get the job done. Not all of these methods may be comfortable for the leader or team, but they can provide new experiences that will challenge the team's thinking.

As someone new to the group, a facilitator has what I call the "credibility of the unknown." A facilitator will be treated differently, and sometimes with more deference than the leader, simply because the facilitator is unknown. (This is similar to how children act better with a new adult than they do responding to their own familiar parents). The team will see the facilitator at the front of the room, which sets them up as an authority. But it doesn't know the rules or how the facilitator operates. This enhances the facilitator's ability to introduce various topics, guide discussions, and tackle the topics that are important to you as a leader.

Remember that when using a facilitator, you are still the leader of the group. There may be questions only you can answer, and your team will still look to you for direction and decision on how the results of the facilitated session will be used.

Using a facilitator is not something you need to do on a regular basis. Ultimately, you are the leader. But it can be a useful tool when you want to take on a difficult issue, shake up your team, or explore a contentious topic.

55. Coaching for Advanced Success

I fully admit that I am biased as I write this next section. I am the leadership coach for entrepreneurs and executives, and I encourage you to consider coaching in support of your growth as a leader.

I was walking with my daughter on a lovely winter day. It had been quite warm the previous few days, resulting in many areas with ice on the pathways and sidewalks. As we crossed each slippery patch, my daughter took my hand, and together we were much more stable. Together we were able to walk confidently and help each other cross icy obstacles. She would steady me when I was unsure of my footing and I would steady her when her foot occasionally slipped.

Amazingly, we rarely, if ever, slipped out of balance at the same time. On my own, I was sure to fall, but together we were able to stabilize one another.

A coach is someone who can help steady you when your feet slip on that icy patch. A coach is someone to get you back on track with your goals. A coach can accelerate progress and has become a common member of a successful leaders' team.

Having a Coach Is Becoming the Standard Business Practice

The International Coaching Federation has conducted research on the coaching industry. From 2015 to 2019, the estimated increase of coaches available was 33%. What is more interesting is that an increasing number of professionals are engaging coaches in their work. The same research estimates that the number of leaders engaging a coach has increased by 46% over this period. And the use of coaching is not restricted to North America but was reported in 161 countries in 2019. It's easy to see that companies, professionals, and businesspeople are reaping the rewards of coaching.

Guru Versus Coach

When I begin coaching a prospective client, I am often asked about my program. They want to know the details of the process. They want a curriculum plan.

This makes sense when you think that a majority of people have come through a highly structured learning environment where everything is planned out for them based on the desires of the person teaching. It's called school.

This learning method continues as adults. Instead of teachers in a schoolroom, we have what I like to call Gurus. A guru is a person who has seen success (or sells the idea of success) and claims to have found the secret to success. For purposes of our comparison, I will not refer to the claimants who defraud others with false promises. Instead, I want to focus on real gurus. These are people who have genuinely had success and want to see others succeed. They often offer courses on how to create the same success in your life as they created in theirs. The training has value, but there is a fundamental difference between this approach and coaching.

A guru will show you their formula for success. A coach will help you find <u>your formula for success</u>. I once heard marketing master Seth Godin interviewed for a podcast, and he affirmed this very idea. He is often sought out for his expertise and insight, yet he is hesitant to share his methods as he has seen such diversity in how people succeed and knows they all have their own strengths and passions that will contribute to their success in their own unique way.

If you want to find <u>a</u> formula for success, learn from a guru. If you want to find <u>your</u> formula for success, hire a coach.

WHY WORK WITH A COACH?

Consistency

There are many different ways to learn. You may have invested in a weekend course, taken an online workshop, or attended an evening speaker. Most people reading this probably attended school, at the very least. In our modern world, we are blessed with an abundance of learning opportunities. Unfortunately, the lessons rarely stick with us.

Learning Solutions Magazine was curious about the question of how much that is taught is actually retained by the person attending a learning opportunity. The results were staggering. In the first hour alone, learners only retain 50% of the material learned. After 48 hours, 75% of the material is forgotten, and in one week the person who sat in the course retains only 10% of what they learned.

I once heard a speaker tell us that we should focus on gaining one nugget of wisdom from his speech. At the time, I thought this was ridiculous. Why only one nugget when I can take in so much more. After years of speaking and listening to other speakers, I now understand that his "one nugget of wisdom" is the 10% of what I retained from the speech. It doesn't seem like much for the amount of time I've committed.

Let's review what happens at most learning opportunities. You attend a great workshop or motivational speaker on the weekend. By the end of it, you feel like a changed person. Unfortunately, you have not transformed your life. In fact, your life is the same. You get up to go back to your current routine and within a week or less the fervor for change you felt has evaporated, and you are back to the life you've been practicing.

This is why it is so powerful to engage with a coach. The process of change is not usually instantaneous so much as a result of ongoing work. It's a result of the steps you take, not the leaps that result in real progress. This is what makes coaching so powerful. It provides regular feedback, reflection, and accountability. A workshop will provide information, but it does not offer these three activities, which are the tools for real change. Coaching does.

JoHari

Joseph Luft and Harrington Ingham created a simple model for describing development in 1955. Using parts of their first names, they call it The Johari Window. It is still relevant today as an insight model based on what you know and don't know about yourself and what others know and do not know about you. Working with a coach can help to illuminate areas of yourself that are unknown or blind spots and thereby help you to grow beyond a current challenge.

Purposeful Practice

You have probably heard the phrase that practice makes perfect. As it turns out, that is only half the equation. Practice is essential, but practicing the right activities are how you gain real expertise. Ericcson and Pool, in their book on high-performance activities, titled *Peak*, call it Purposeful Practice.

The natural question that follows is, "How do I know what to practice?" This is where coaching comes into relevance. Every star athlete, every great musician, every top performer has had someone in their life who has served as a coach or mentor. This person has helped shape their growth by providing the insight of experience to guide the activities that will push this person to the next level of their skill.

You don't need a coach to practice. You are able to do this on your own. In fact, most practice is done individually. But knowing what to practice will prevent you from staying at the same level of competence. Contrary to popular belief, practicing the same thing a thousand times doesn't make you a thousand times better unless you are practicing very specific activities. You may practice your small talk, which is great if you are uncomfortable networking, but if you want to move beyond this, it is useful to have someone who will analyze where your strengths are as you improve and have you focus on very specific activities—perhaps your introduction, linking others to the conversation, eye contact, body posture, etc. One of the coach's roles is to help identify the activities that will make your practice purposeful in order to support skill advancement.

Speed of Learning

We are blessed with the ability to learn. It is one of the core values of being human. Though we can all learn on our own, it is much faster to learn with others.

When was young, I had the benefit of attending a basketball camp. It was a week long. Over the course of that week, we practiced drills, played games, watched instructional videos, and worked one-on-one with a coach. It was a lot of fun, and it was also when I realized the benefit of having someone outside myself giving me feedback.

I was an average basketball player, and the one skill I was struggling with is fundamental to the sport—shooting the basketball. During the camp, my coach told me to bring my feet closer together. My stance was too wide. I sincerely listened and believed I was applying the feedback. Being a good coach, he could tell I hadn't changed my bad habit, so he upped his game and videotaped me taking ten shots. Afterward, we watched them together. He pointed out the correction he recommended, and I could see for myself what I was doing. This was very powerful. It helped me to realize and actualize the feedback. Seeing myself perform was more powerful than being told what to do. As a result, I practiced narrowing my stance and I became a better shooter.

If I didn't have a coach, I might never have realized I had a bad habit holding me back. Moreover, without a persistent coach, I may never have changed what I was doing. We only worked on this for an hour on one of the days of the camp. In one hour, I was able to learn enough to improve. On my own, my learning process would have been a lot slower, or I may never have learned it. With a coach, it sped up my ability to learn, adapt, and improve my skills.

Accountability

Having someone to whom you are accountable is a powerful motivational tool. When I was in graduate school, I decided that I wanted to relearn how to swim. I had some ear issues in my younger days, and as a result, I lost my connection to the water. Fortunately, I had a classmate who swam competitively and offered to teach me how to swim.

We agreed to swim in the morning. The trick was that we had to go early because of our class and work schedules, which meant we had to leave our apartments very early to get to the pool.

Each morning, I would call my friend, Mike, and we would go swimming. We went regularly but occasionally I missed our lesson after pulling an all-nighter and catching up on sleep that morning. Guess what Mike did on those days—he slept in too. He was very clear that he would go swimming, but only if I was going. That is exactly how it turned out, and it reinforced a powerful lesson for me. It's easier to move forward with my goals when working with someone else. Together we went to the pool. Individually, we both failed to get our morning swim.

Working with a coach or mentor is much like my swim lessons with Mike. Regular follow up provides the accountability to keep moving forward. I know a lot of people who want to write a book. Very few have started, let alone completed one. Those that have, usually have someone else as part of their team—motivating, supporting, and challenging them to succeed.

What if What You See Was Always Possible?

Think back on a busy time in your life. Perhaps there was a challenge or a series of challenging circumstances. Maybe you had a major project and had no idea how you were going to complete it. You may have felt in a difficult place financially, finally choosing to make changes to improve this situation.

Regardless of the circumstance, think about what it was like when you got past it. How had you grown? In what ways were you stronger? How did your world, or your outlook on your world, improve?

Consider this: What if the positive change you experienced was always possible? What if it could have happened sooner? Sometimes it is hard to believe in a bright future, especially in the midst of a difficult moment. Yet, that future was always possible.

Why does a coach get paid so much?

Sometimes potential clients only see the cost of coaching without understanding or seeing the value of coaching. You may wonder why coaches charge the fees they do. The following are all considerations that go into determining coaching fees.

- You aren't getting one hour of the coach's training. You are gaining the benefit of the thousands of dollars of training and years of experience the coach brings to that one hour to help you accelerate your growth.
- The fee is a good indicator of the coach's sense of self-worth. Do you want to hire a coach that doesn't value themselves? If a coach does not value their services enough to price it, what value are you expecting to get from their service?
- A coach is 100% dedicated to you. They are not on your staff. They are not your competition. They provide a confidential relationship where you can share everything and know that it is kept confidential. What is it worth to you to have one relationship in your life where you know the other person is 100% there for you—no judgement and no agenda because

you are the agenda.

- A coach will challenge you. A coach will tell you what you don't want to hear. Those around you may only tell you good news, not because they are dishonest, but because they don't want to risk their jobs. A coach will tell you, as there is nothing to lose.

- Engaging a coach is not about what it costs you. It is about what it will give you. There are numerous examples of businesspeople focusing solely on the cost of something and disregarding the potential. If coaching cost you $50,000 this year, but you increased the revenue of your company by $5,000,000, was it worth it? More importantly, if you change in a significant way that allows you to grow your business bigger or improve your quality of life and relationships, what is that worth to you? The result is priceless. The cost, no matter how much, is irrelevant to the result.

- Coaching is transformational, and true coaching is customized for each person. No two people are the same. No two people have the same life experience, mental habits, or challenges. Coaching is about you. If it's not, then you're not truly being coached.

- It looks like you're paying for an hour or however long the program is. What you are paying for is all of the work that you don't see. A coach spends time in planning, preparation, and reflection before and after client meetings. It's like going out to a restaurant. The price does not reflect only the cost of food. It pays for the wait staff and cooks. It covers the utility bills, property tax, and all of the other expenses to run that restaurant. A good coach gets paid well for all the work that happens outside the meeting to create a transformational experience in the meeting.

- I Already Got My Education

According to Maclean's, the average annual cost for post-secondary education in 2018 was $19,498.75. Let's round that to an even $20,000. That is $20,000 multiplied by four years of education, which means on average a post-secondary student is spending $80,000 to attain their degree. Yet, many of the skills they will need are developed on the job.

Some may choose other ways to educate themselves such as attending a course, weekend training, or motivational event from a prominent public speaker. They may pay $1000, $5000, $10,000, even $50,000 for one event. If you've had the privilege of enrolling in events such as these, how did you feel during the event? Was the course amazing? Were you inspired to change your life? Were you certain that immediately after this event everything would be different, only to have Monday come and see yourself back in the habits you've established?

Consider the money you've spent on education, training, and development. How much did you get out of these experiences? Do you feel fundamentally transformed, or was it simply money spent. What if you could get real transformative change in your life? What would it be worth to you to have a personal coach for your work, your business, your mind, your life? You may have gotten an education, but did you get transformation?

BE THE LEADER YOU'RE MEANT TO BE; LIVE LIKE A LEADER

It is not the critic who counts; not the man [or woman] who points out how the strong man [or woman] stumbles, or where the doer of deeds could have done them better. The credit belongs to the man [or woman] who is actually in the arena, whose face is marred by dust and sweat and blood; who strives valiantly; who errs, who comes short again and again, because there is no effort without error and shortcoming; but who does actually strive to do the deeds.

— Theodore Roosevelt

56. Be the Boss

Even as you ask your team for their opinion, always remember: They Want You to Be the Boss!

Not everyone is ready to take on the responsibility you've chosen. In fact, many absolutely do not want the level of responsibility that comes with being a leader.

Have you ever noticed that the hardest position to fill on any volunteer board is that of President? I've worked with individuals who are amazing and give extraordinarily of themselves, yet they will not take on the responsibility of that top role. They do not want to be the one who has to make the tough decisions, have difficult conversations, or face the consequences of those actions.

Those you lead want you to be that person. They want you to be the one who will make the decision that no one wants to make. They want you to be the person who will respond to the angry supervisor, colleague, parent, client, customer when that person feels somehow wronged. Even if they think they know how your area should be run, they will never step up to take the responsibility required to do so.

Leadership is a lot like parenting. Your child doesn't need you to be another buddy or friend for them. It's not that you will not be friendly with your child, but they need you to be their parent. It is a role only you can fill. Being the boss is similar. You can be friendly, inclusive, and supportive; but your team still needs you to be the boss.

Being the boss isn't about power tripping, insecurity, coercion, or ego. It is about being a confident and present leader that trusts your team while being able to make decisions. Though humans work well with autonomy, they still want the structure of knowing who the boss is. This is your job. Be the boss.

Appendix

The appendix includes two topics that are useful to leaders but didn't fit elsewhere in the book.

57. Leading During Challenging Times

In my previous career, I had the privilege of leading an outstanding team through two very challenging crises in our community. Both situations created a need for emergency housing for fellow citizens in the province of Alberta. From these experiences, powerful lessons were learned that are applicable whenever leaders are experiencing challenging times.

The first emergency occurred in 2013 when the Bow River, which flows through the middle of Calgary, Alberta, rose to 100-year epic levels. The downtown shut down, and it was estimated that more than 100,000 people were displaced from their homes.

In a city of one million people, it is significant when your downtown stops for business. As you can imagine, for many others it is even more significant when you are unable to stay in your home. For those who were displaced, the university residence program that my team and I managed became their new temporary home.

The second emergency arose when, in 2016, wildfires threatened to burn up areas of populated northern Alberta. As a pre-emptive measure, thousands of people were evacuated to other parts of the province. Once again, my team was called upon to house those needing shelter, and we managed to help over 1800 people in their time of need.

At first glance, it may seem that these two crises are distinctly different. One was caused by water and the other by fire. Yet, at the core of the response was providing short-term emergency housing to individuals and families. The lessons learned that made each experience successful were surprisingly similar, and they can be useful when dealing with emergencies that arrive on any scale in your company, department, or team.

Communicate as Much as You Can as Soon as You Can

Though it is useful to take the time to craft key messaging when communicating externally, it is more important to communicate with your staff directly and swiftly in an emergency. I recommend erring on the side of overcommunication. It is better for everyone to feel a part of the response than to have confusion due to their not communicating enough or at all.

In these emergencies, I began the very first night by drafting a simple bullet point email to my team, updating them on the current situation. It included any change to a policy or member of the response team (we had many partner organizations, and the team needed to know with whom they would be working), confirmation of the next operations meeting, and the status of any outstanding decisions.

Tell Them What You Don't Know

It is important to share what has changed, but also, the team will often have questions and will be curious as to the answers. Be sure to share what you don't know. Otherwise, they will make up their own stories, and this can create confusion too. Telling them what you don't know:

- Acknowledges the concerns and demonstrates that you are paying attention to what is being said, discussed, or gossiped about. Further, it ensures that they will continue to bring up issues, ideas, and trends because they feel heard. This is a huge asset, as you will be able to find and adapt to concerns much more quickly than in an environment of closed communication.
- Affirms and calms the staff, knowing that the topic is being addressed and understanding where it is in terms of resolution. When the team knows their questions will be answered, it gets them out of survival mode and allows them to focus on those they are responsible to help.
- Prevents gossip, false stories, and rumors. Unlike fake news, your team will have the real news and this allows them to better respond to the situation and represent your organization in a reputable way.

This process of a daily update became so useful that it was co-opted outside my team for use by our colleagues coordinating the university's response. It was a great tool that helped the entire broader team respond in a positive and highly impactful way.

Never Assume the Current Problem Is Your Only Problem

The primary problem when providing emergency housing on short notice is to prepare clean rooms in which individuals and families can stay. Naturally, that was the focus of our attention. We soon learned that, although this was THE problem, it was not the only problem.

During the floods, we thought we were only providing housing. Yet, we were providing housing to a broad range of citizens, which means we had everyone from families to drug users living next to one another. This required us to collaborate with police services, coordinate special cleaning of rooms, and coordinate alternate housing options.

When the wildfires drove people to us in that emergency, we soon learned that a gastrointestinal virus was afflicting some of those in housing. We now had to adapt and track illness, engage the next level of cleaning protocol, and implement isolation measures, including food delivery, in order to meet the basic needs of the evacuees staying with us.

Though you don't need to go in depth when debriefing your team in an emergency, take some time to ask this question:

Now that we have dealt with everything we need to respond to for this emergency, what are we possibly missing, or what problem or consideration may arise in the next few days or beyond?

It is powerful to remind your team that you still need to think ahead. No one is prescient but asking them to look ahead will help all of them to think about this emergency in a new way.

People Will Take Care of Themselves

When an emergency strikes, we sometimes think that we have to plan to take care of everyone in our community. Depending on the emergency, the majority of people will probably take care of themselves. Of all the people displaced by flood and fire, we housed less than 2000 in each event. Where did the rest of the people go?

They took care of themselves. Those with recreational vehicles started camping out. Folks stayed with friends or family. Many were in hotels with the support of their insurance. As a result, only a fraction of residents needed our services.

When planning for an emergency, consider how you can help people help themselves. They want to take action in solving their current problem. How can you support this?

Support Your Team's Need to Care for Their Families

In times of crisis, our vision narrows to our own welfare and that of our families. Support your team by caring for their families. Once this has been done, you will receive a great amount of focus and motivation from them in return. Caring for family is like taking in a breath; until your team does this, they will not be able to breathe again or focus on what you need them to do.

Navigating

At the time of this writing, every business, every community, and indeed every person is responding to the COVID-19 pandemic. If you thought you might never experience a high-level emergency like this, you may be wondering how to respond. Start by considering how you will communicate. Organize your resources and thrive during this challenging time, and you will be able to thrive during any challenge.

58. A Common Leadership Challenge

Not dealing with issues is like drinking poison and expecting the other person to get sick.

— Paraphrased from Glenda Staples

Though it may feel lonely at times, as a leader you will rarely experience a situation unique from other leaders. Leadership, at its core, is about relationships. As such, similar problems arise across different organizations, businesses, and communities. In support of this, I have responded to a common concern that leaders have shared with me, to offer a perspective on how to deal with it.

Why do I have to hold my staff members' hands?

This is a great question and sums up a common source of much frustration for leaders. It can be very disappointing when we see slow change or no change in a colleague, especially when trying to implement a new policy, project, or practice. It is common to question their initiative and ask why they aren't learning and applying knowledge faster. Here are some possibilities for answering this question that might help reduce your frustration and improve the situation.

Lack of Communication

Change takes time. Mentioning a new idea once is not enough to have the idea stick with the members of your team.

How did you introduce this idea to your team?

How do you know they understood what you told them?

How can you reinforce the change you seek?

Have you written down your expectations?

Leaders get busy. When time is crunched, it is easy to assume that your team members think as you do. You may believe you told them of your expectations, but have you written them down in a place where you and your team members can all refer to them?

As you write out your expectations, you receive the first benefit because it forces you to clarify your thoughts. What you have rattling around in your mind often comes out differently when written on paper. If you can clarify your objectives, it will make it much easier to communicate and see them realized with your team.

Having written expectations is a great help to your team as well. It gives each of you a common reference point and reduces confusion. Instead of each person interpreting your spoken words differently, providing the written form increases the likelihood of shared understanding.

Lack of Training

Often a leader will tell their team of a desired change. You may have been thinking of this idea for some time, and it is easy to forget that your team is hearing it for the first time. They will need time to process and adapt to the idea. It's easy to expect them to embrace the new idea as it makes perfect sense to you. It is important; however, to realize that training is needed; this idea may not yet make sense to them.

People learn in stages and through experience. Too often, leaders focus on a training system that tells their staff what to do or how to use a new system. This can be an acceptable first step, but it is imperative not to end the training here. One-time training is not enough to effect change.

The next phase of the training happens after the team begins to apply the new system or idea. Using the system now becomes real to them. They are learning in a hands-on environment, and this is when many questions will arise. In the initial training they may not know what to ask. Once they begin using the new system, that is when they will have questions.

To ensure the team is learning the new process, have them show you what they know. As they demonstrate the process to you, you will see the gaps and misunderstandings. If you assume that they know, you will usually be disappointed. Having the team members show you what they've learned accelerates their further learning and saves time; it is easier for you to train them on their specific areas of difficulty rather than giving another generalized training.

The final phase comes as the team has been trained and begun to apply the change in their workplace. This is the time to debrief the team and create a shared learning to reinforce the change and make it the default for your operation rather than this "new thing" the boss wants to do.

Accountability

Another pitfall for leaders is to expect change in their team without requiring any accountability in the team for making the change.

I was working with Paulo, who runs a drafting team. Quality Control was important to him as their weakness in this area had caused numerous headaches and back charges with clients. Through our coaching process, he decided on a procedure – a checklist, really – that would reduce the variance in the final product and create consistency in their operations.

Paulo designed a great checklist. It was perfect for improving their final product to the client.

Two weeks after implementing the new checklist, Paulo was frustrated. He learned that his team was not using the checklist. He told them about it and showed it to them, but that was not enough for them to adopt it.

Where Paulo fell down was in failing to hold his team accountable for using the checklist. This is a new procedure, and most people like to use what they already know, not something new. In order for the change to stick, there needs to be accountability for its use. Here are some actions Paulo took to improve the use of the checklist:

At his daily briefings, he asked about each project related to the checklist.

When a document was submitted for final review, he asked to see the checklist attached to it.

He followed up with the leaders on his team asking them how they are using the list and teaching their teams to use it.

Cloning

Are you expecting your staff to be a clone of you? One tenet of basic human dynamics is that we like those who are like us. Robert Chialdini noted this in his book, *Influence: The Psychology of Persuasion*. It is one of the reasons people interviewing for a job or pitching an investment are advised to dress similarly to the people to whom they are presenting.

At work and in business, similarity manifests not just in what we look like, but also in wanting people to operate as we do. Although our team can learn from us and may adapt some of our practices, each person is unique. How each person approaches a task will vary. Are you more concerned with how a task is done or the results achieved? When you focus on results, it opens a world of possibility as to how it is achieved. If you are struggling, is it because your staff member isn't operating the way you would or because they are not achieving the desired results?

Change Takes Time

Inevitably, change takes time. More importantly, it takes a commitment from the leader. The leader needs to invest time at the front of the process to ensure that a new protocol or practice is learned, adopted, and institutionalized within the organization. The good news is that once you have established this new practice with your team, you no longer need to spend time managing the change. It has now become part of your common expectation within the work environment, and the team can support new colleagues when they come on board.

To use an analogy, managing a change as a leader is a lot like cooking a meal. For most meals, the majority of time is spent on the preparation of the food---shopping for groceries, washing vegetables, gathering spices, chopping, and cooking the ingredients. The actual eating of the meal is the easiest and least time-consuming aspect of the food cycle. Change is similar. It takes a lot of investment in time upfront, but once this is done, the rest is easy.

Further Reading and Resources

Camp, Jim. Start With NO. New York, New York: Crown Business, 2002.

Ericcson, A. & Pool, R. Peak: Secrets from the New Science of Expertise. Eamon Dolan/Houghton Mifflin Harcourt: 2016.

Franklin, D. & Andrews, J. Megachange: The World in 2050. Hoboken, NJ: John Wiley & Sons, 2012.

Hero With a Thousand Faces. Documentary: 2016.

International Coaching Federation. 2020 ICF Global Coaching Study. 2020.

Kohn, Art. Brain Science: The Forgetting Curve – the Dirty Secret of Corporate Training. https://learningsolutionsmag.com/articles/1379/brain-science-the-forgetting-curvethe-dirty-secret-of-corporate-training

Kraus MW, Huang C, Keltner D. Tactile communication, cooperation, and performance: an ethological study of the NBA. Emotion. 2010;10(5):745-749. doi:10.1037/a0019382

Maclean's article on the cost of a post-secondary education. https://www.macleans.ca/education/the-cost-of-a-canadian-university-education-in-six-charts/

Nelson, Noelle. Make More Money by Making Your Employees

Happy. MindLab Publishing, 2012.

Origin of hard skills versus soft skills.
https://en.wikipedia.org/wiki/Soft_skills

Public Health Agency of Canada. COVID-19 in Canada: Using data and modelling to inform public health action. April 9, 2020. https://www.canada.ca/content/dam/phac-aspc/documents/services/diseases/2019-novel-coronavirus-infection/using-data-modelling-inform-eng.pdf

Sharot, Tali. The Influential Mind: What the Brain Reveals About Our Power to Change Others. Henry Holt and Company, 2017.

Skills Employees Want to See in Their Bosses.
https://learning.linkedin.com/blog/learning-tips/the--1-quality-people-want-in-a-manager-is-?trk=edpartner_Inc.BossDay_learning&src=s-other

Social Market Foundation. Happiness and productivity: Understanding the happy-productive worker. Accessed August 3, 2020. http://www.smf.co.uk/wp-content/uploads/2015/10/Social-Market-Foundation-Publication-Briefing-CAGE-4-Are-happy-workers-more-productive-281015.pdf#page=9

Willink, Jocko & Babin, Leif. Extreme Ownership: How U.S. Navy SEALS Lead and Win. St. Martin's Press, 2015.

www.ingramcontent.com/pod-product-compliance
Lightning Source LLC
Chambersburg PA
CBHW072006110526
44592CB00012B/1218